CULTURE
&
IDENTITY

Vol.1 - WORLD

Poetry exploring culture and identity, from
poets around the world.

Compiled by Robin Barratt

THE POET

A leading international online poetry magazine, recognized for both its themed collections, and its interviews with poets worldwide; looking at their work and their words, and what motivates and inspires them to write.

www.ThePoetMagazine.org

~

CULTURE & IDENTITY
Vol.1 - WORLD

Published by THE POET

ISBN: 9798414877431

E: Robin@ThePoetMagazine.org

Cover image and design: Canva
www.Canva.com

Compiled and published for THE POET by:
Robin Barratt Publishing
Affordable Publishing Services

www.RobinBarratt.co.uk

THE POET is sponsored by:

www.PoemsOverCoffee.com

"John Johnson is a proud sponsor of THE POET."

If you would also like to sponsor THE POET, please go to:

www.thepoetmagazine.org/support-us

ALSO FROM THE POET

We produce some of the largest international anthologies on particular themes and topics ever published.

ADVERSITY: Volumes 1 & 2
FRIENDS & FRIENDSHIP: Volumes 1 & 2
FAITH: Volumes 1 & 2
CHILDHOOD: Volumes 1 & 2
CHRISTMAS – SPECIAL EDITION
A NEW WORLD - Rethinking our lives post-pandemic.
ON THE ROAD: Volumes 1 & 2
WAR & BATTLE
THE SEASONS
LOVE

CONTENTS

159. Kakoli Ghosh - INDIA
161. Neil Leadbeater - SCOTLAND
165. Masudul Hoq - BANGLADESH
167. Eduard Schmidt-Zorner - REPUBLIC OF IRELAND / GERMANY
175. Ivana Radojičić - SERBIA
179. John Tunaley - ENGLAND
181. Tanja Ajtic - CANADA / SERBIA
185. Aminath Neena - MALDIVES
189. Claudia Hardt - BAHRAIN / GERMANY
191. Chester Civelli - SWITZERLAND
195. Prof. Ron Roman - SOUTH KOREA
197. Rozalia Aleksandrova - BULGARIA
199. Zorica Bajin Đukanović - SERBIA
203. Volkan Hacıoğlu - TURKEY
205. Hussein Habasch - KURDISTAN / GERMANY
209. Tessa Thomson - ENGLAND
211. David A Banks - ENGLAND
213. Bhuwan Thapaliya - NEPAL
217. William Khalipwina Mpina - MALAWI
219. P. J. Reed - ENGLAND
221. George David - ROMANIA
225. Irma Kurti - ITALY / ALBANIA
229. Bill Cox - SCOTLAND
231. Dr. Ana Stjelja - SERBIA
233. Nivedita Karthik - INDIA
237. Ayesha Khurram - PAKISTAN
239. Rema Tabangcura - PHILIPPINES / SINGAPORE
243. Raji Unnikrishnan - BAHRAIN / INDIA
245. Kate Young - ENGLAND
249. Amrita Valan - INDIA
255. Alicia Minjarez Ramírez - MEXICO
259. Maja Herman-Sekuli - SERBIA
263. Maria Editha Garma-Respicio - HONG KONG / PHILIPPINES
265. Brajesh Singh - INDIA
267. James Aitchison - AUSTRALIA
269. Dr. Rehmat Changaizi - PAKISTAN
273. Alun Robert - ENGLAND
275. Ion-Marius Tatomir - ROMANIA
277. Mary Anne Zammit - MALTA
281. Monica Manolachi - ROMANIA
285. Igor Pop Trajkov - REPUBLIC OF NORTH MACEDONIA
289. Tanya A. Nikolova - BULGARIA
291. Miroslava Panayotova - BULGARIA
295. Ewith Bahar - INDONESIA
299. Kathleen Boyle - VIETNAM / ENGLAND
303. Aleksandra Vujisić - MONTENEGRO

307. Máire Malone - ENGLAND / REPUBLIC OF IRELAND
309. Prafull Shiledar - INDIA
313. Tatyana Savova Yotova - BULGARIA
315. Dr. Sarah Clarke - ENGLAND
319. Shaswata Gangopadhyay - INDIA
321. Julie Ann Tabigne - SINGAPORE / PHILIPPINES
323. Dr. Archana Bahadur Zutshi - INDIA

"Cultural identity is a part of a person's identity, or their self-conception and self-perception, and is related to nationality, ethnicity, religion, social class, generation, locality or any kind of social group that has its own distinct culture."

J.P. Sexton
REPUBLIC OF IRELAND

J.P. Sexton grew up on the Inishowen peninsula of Co. Donegal. He started writing whilst attending St. Patrick's primary school in Carndonagh. His humble beginnings included living with his brothers and sisters in several thatch cottages, and even a double-decker bus, none of which had running water, and some not even electricity. His writing reflects on those early days and on the characters he met along the way. In 2014 he published his first memoir titled; *The Big Yank - Memoir of a Boy Growing Up Irish*. In 2018, along with two other author friends, he published a collection of Irish stories called; *Four Green Fields; Wild Irish Banter & Stories,Shenanigans and Poetry*. He has been published in *The Irish Times, The Garda Review* and *The Connaught Telegraph*. He is currently editing a memoir sequel; *Drawn to Danger* (working title). His poetry and fiction is heavily influenced by the Irish landscape, its people and their stories.
E: jp@irishauthor.us
W: www.irishauthor.us
FB: @john.sexton169

MY ISLAND

I have no need
of a back cassock
reminder
to bend a knee
and give thanks.

The wind
whispers to me
when the wild horses
of Manannan mac Lir
thunder ashore in Malin Head

or the sand dunes
around Lagg
beckon
as they did
to me as a boy.

My Island
speaks to me
in ways
a missionary
never could.

She knows
that I listen
and respect
her present and past.
For she is me

and I am her.

MY ROAD

Saw a quote
about roads
and one
less travelled.

No need
to wonder
why many
wander the other.

The path
of my journey
is overgrown.
I must machete my way through.

Twists and turns
it heaves and churns
like a currach
in a gale.

My road
has seas
dark and wild
like a Donegal night.

I stay on my road
for it leads me.
Even when it bleeds me,
it is my road

to the end.

WAITING

Waiting for a dry spell
to cut
the hay
knowing that a spell
may be
but a day.

Dear bought work
small farm
in Donegal.
Cattle feeder
winter heater
one cap fits all.

"When's the best time
to visit Ireland?"
asks the tourist.
"when it's not raining"
says I
like some weather Jedi.

And still
the small farmer waits
as one never knows
when fine days chose
to stop by
with a few of their mates.

Christopher Okemwa
KENYA

Christopher has a PhD in performance poetry from Moi University, Kenya, and is a literature lecturer. He is the founder and current director of Kistrech International Poetry festival in Kenya. His novella, *Sabina and the Mystery of the Ogre*, won the Canadian Burt Award for African Literature in 2015. Its sequel, *Sabina the Rain Girl* (Nsemia Inc., 2019) was selected for the UN SDG 2 Zero Hunger reading list in 2021. Okemwa is the editor of *Musings During a Time of Pandemic: A World Anthology of Poems on COVID-19*, *I Can't Breathe: A Poetic Anthology of Social Justice* and *The Griots of Ubuntu: An Anthology of Contemporary Poetry from Africa.* He has written nine books of poetry and been translated to Armenian, Chinese, Greek, Norwegian, Finnish, Hungarian, Arabic, Polish, Chinese, Nepalese, Turkish, Russian, Spanish, Catalan, Dutch and Serbian. Christopher has also translated four literary works of international poets from English to Swahili, and is the author of ten folktales of the Abagusii people of Kenya, three children's storybooks, one play, two novels and four oral literature textbooks.
E: chris@okemwa.co.ke
W: www.okemwa.co.ke
W: www.kistrechpoetry.org

MUST YOU TELL YOUR MOTHER?
(A Poem for the Warriors in Our Community)

When the war has began
Must you tell your mother?
You coward
You dog of a boy!
A curse to the community
A shame to the young generation
Must you tell your mother?
Must you?
Must you tell your mother?

When the battle-horn has been blown
And the village stirs
Women gather arrows and line up spears
Their men paint themselves in ochre and in soot
Must you linger about?
Must you be undecidedly confused?
Must you turn your head back to your mama?
What kind are you?
Whose tit did you suckle?
Who reared you in her nest?
Which knife cut your foreskin?
Oh little coward boy
Must you?
Must you tell your mother?

When the battle-drum has been beaten
And the warriors are lined up for death and for life
And the enemy is lurking about in the forest
Should you seek advice from your mother?
Should you?
Should you look back to find your mother?
Oh coward of cowards
A curse of curses
Should you seek for your mother?

When the other lads are out
Drums reverberating
Dancers quaking the ground on the ridges
Cows bellowing
Goats bleating
The fields awash with crops

And the people talking in innuendoes
Must you lag behind?
Must you be in the hut warming your egesena?
Oh coward of cowards
A curse of curses
Should you lag behind?
Should you tell your mother?

NOTE: Egesena, a traditional piece of cloth in the Abagusii community in Kenya tied around the waist to cover the front part of the person's private parts.

WHEN I DIE

When I die
Do not hold back those tears
Let them flow freely
To wet your youthful face
Like rain water

When I die
Wriggle on the dusty ground
And beat the dry soil with your bare hands
Shout and scream
Remember - you are bereaved!
Tear your clothes in anguish
Uproot your hair in agony
Bite your skin
Let blood ooze out

When I am no more
Sit late under the moonlight
And beat the drums
Pluck the obokano strings
Blow the family horn
Let people run down from the hillside
Hurry up from the valleys
Let them moan with you
And help with the misfortunes

When I breathe no more
Mourn like a really African woman
Destroy the food crops
Cut down the banana plants
Uproot the maize plants
Destroy the sugar canes
Dismantle them in fury

Like a true African woman
Run through the market place
Shouting my name
My father's name
My grandfather's name
The entire family lineage
Let them know your tribulations
Clutch their cheeks in sympathy

Gape in amazement

After the day of the amatati
Let the in-laws and relatives come in
With spears, shields, ekeboye, ekegwora
Chase away the spirits of death
Dwelling in our home

Let them dress the cows in egwagwa
Drive them to the grave site
As they bellow a dirge
Let them lock horns in grief
As they perform eburu dance

Once the eburu day is finished
Let the owls gather in the evening
On the hedgerows
To hoot a desolate orchestra
Let mysterious black cats assemble
At the door-step of our house
With a mixture of doleful purrs

NOTES:
Amatati - the nuclear family (eg siblings, parents, uncle, aunt, cousins) who are allowed to bury the dead person on the burial day.
Eburu - A ceremony performed for the dead person a day after amatati have done the burial. It is attended by in-laws, relatives and other people. On this day cows are brought to the grave to dance, in-laws and relatives chase death in a mockery fight using clubs (e.g. ekeboye and ekeguora), spears and shields.
Ekeguora - A long club
Ekeboye - A short and heavy club
Egwagwa - Plants (climbers) wrapped round the cows as they perform eburu dance (a burial dance)

First published in *The Pieta*, translated to Armenian by Hermine Navasardyan, sponsored by Sona Van, 2019.

Tony Frisby
ENGLAND

Tony the author of five poetry collections. From the age of 19, he dropped out of school in Waterford (Republic of Ireland), and emigrated to England. After dedicating himself to many informal and service jobs, and achieving some financial solvency, he returned to academic education in the late 1980s. He graduated from Brunel with an MA in Modern Literature, and subsequently did a PhD in Irish Poetry.
FB: @tony.frisby.1

NEITHER HERE NOR THERE

Between nations, between desires,
between the warm glow of memory
and the colding embers of here and now,
between crinkle-cut Kodak snapshots
of rain-soaked outings to Tramore Strand,

and knife-sharp, digital images
of yet another place that isn't
Ballybricken Square, I dither in an ocean
of indecision; flounder between
the here of 'now' and a 'then', of soft,

sepia recall; no raft, no tide or current
to ferry my changeling self,
back to its beginnings or bear the weight
of this nagging, leaden fear,
that the world once known

has changed too many times
upon its green-grassed self, to celebrate
my return with ceilidhs and céad mile fáiltes
on the long-ago summer road
to Dumore East.

A BOREEN IN COUNTY WATERFORD

Cut me deep, slice my blue-black veins
and the flow of blood will taste
of the rivers that brought me from Africa.
 Now I am a stick-man on a cave wall,

a drawer of shimmering images which,
as the ice melts, I leave to delight the gaping future.
Find me again in a bog in Denmark,
note the leather torc, my sacrificed life,

the gold-work around my neck.
Note too my stocky build,
the hair that lines my grinning skull;
its ginger hue still adorns the pates

of my brothers and sisters in the Western Isles.
And though that reign is done,
the world remembers my horned head,
savage axe and Viking tongue,

just as these Sussex Downs
know my lesser sins, the bracken
on Pen Pumlumon Fawr my need of solitude.
But only the Celt in me knows

the march of Alba, the ache of conquest,
the loss of tongue, the green taste of hunger,
those coffin ships, the deaths of heroes,
that double yoke of religion.

*

And so it is that, though my tent
is now firmly set upon an English coast
it's a boreen in County Waterford that knows me best;
hip and haw, old man's beard,
the woodbine smell of honeysuckle,
the buttery glow of gorse,
remembering the routes already travelled,
the memories accumulated
the sacrifices, the changes made.

Only here is my future known,
my needs understood, here,
amongst the Fuchsias, dancing
in a boreen in County Waterford.

Zohreh Baghban
IRAN

Zohreh - pen name Raha.M - is a 33 year-old Iranian currently living in Tehran. She is fluent in English and Farsi, and holds an MA in English Lit. from Allame Tabataba'i University in Tehran. Her interests are animal studies, climate change, literature and art, and dabbles in mixed-media art.
E: zohrehspidy@gmail.com
W: www.openendedlit.wordpress.com
Twitter: @RahaM03917673

YESTERDAY

I was born yesterday
when the blossoms blew in the wind
where the birds kissed
when parts of speech were only complimentary
where distance was only in the hearts.
I was born tomorrow
when nobody lived anymore
where landscapes blew the cities
when language was back on the walls
where force became a legend,
kids grew backwards and forwards grew shame.
I was born today as a blip in the horizon.
my gaze is never answered.

IVY THORNS

Bitten sore spots of ivy thorns,
Bore the smiles worn by sea men on marshes.
Thus spoke dead leaves of days forgotten,
Of hours witnessed by the shrouds, of slaughtering heroism.
Hear me ye young clouds, tonight the skies shall weep for due children of the earth.
For they'll inherit the blood moors!

SOCIAL BRIDGES

Love is pain multiplied by a hundred stab wounds
Aiming at desires, tearing them apart to pieces.
Lost in ambiguous abyss of regards and stares,
Meanings lost.
Life would be a lot less backbreaking
If we told the tale of our hearts first hand.
Commodity of our minds dared not.
Oceans apart his eyes haunt me forever.
Forks on the road tore my limbs but I let the wheels crush me to
speak.
I wish ...
You could see through me ...
My tongue is made only for suffocation.
Knowing a hundred tongues made love all the same Greek to me.
Yearned, instead of ridicule, for the first time for held hands ...
On a ball full of billions and yet I'm on Mars lost among red ashes of
my fleshed sensation ...
Chemistry is not the pull ... just alchemy ...
Happy and madly sad ... now I see what they meant ...

Gabriela Docan
ENGLAND / ROMANIA

Gabriela is a humanist, poet, nature lover, chronic daydreamer, over thinker, traveller, with joy of life and admiration for all things that are beautiful. Many things inspire her to write, such as a memory, a song, a nature walk, a personal experience, people, romantic relationships, inner struggles and her work experience in mental health. Her poems have been published by *Writer's Egg Magazine, Spillwords.com* and various print anthologies.
E: gabriela_docan@yahoo.com

A FORMER LIFE

Cushioned against oppressive chains,
Swiftly sentenced to day dreaming,
I grew up with the sight of mountains
From a grey communist building.

The wire of the rotary dial phone
Corkscrewed and curled like my hair,
Music filled rooms from a *magnetofon,*
Mum knitted and crocheted with flair.

We changed TV channels by hand,
To watch news, cartoons or "Dallas",
In the kitchen candles were in demand,
As power cuts loomed over us.

At school, we rose from wooden benches
To sing the national anthem with pride,
Before deploying giggles and grimaces,
Under which we all felt unified.

We played outside with other children,
Knees were always scratched and bleeding.
At night we were afraid to get eaten
By *Baba Cloanța*, if not sleeping.

When festive seasons started to trumpet,
Compotes and pickles filled winter jars,
Sarmale were rolled like Persian carpets
That were beaten outside on iron bars.

Stuffed peppers, stews, soups, sweet bread
Divinely charmed and warmed senses,
While a war with dust was declared
With crystal glasses and porcelain vases.

Wood cracked inside the terracotta stove,
While snowflakes pressed against windows,
We skated in the middle of the road,
Made snowmen in frozen meadows.

In summertime it was hot and humid,
Our night bloomed with mosquitoes,

To kill them, my dad was not timid -
With pillows or books, making graffito.

We swam in rivers and climbed trees,
Strolled on hills full of wild flowers,
Along railway tracks unafraid, with ease,
As trains crawled with few miles per hour.

We picked mushrooms in the woods,
Played hide and seek among sunflowers,
In the street corners of the neighbourhood,
We gathered to chat in the late hours.

We travelled around on country roads,
Explored counties and nature reserves,
In dad's Dacia car, by trains or boats,
From north to where Black Sea waves.

A LANDSCAPE CORNUCOPIA

The Earth wonderfully lodges
a unique vast ocean of green,
where fairylike mist emerges
from treetops, like a dream.

Mountains and wooden churches,
castles from medieval times
rise from a land that stretches
hypnotically, before one's eyes.

Rivers gush out from mountains
untamed, pristine and carefree,
snaking through forests and plains,
providing wildlife sanctuary.

Underground glaciers, gorges,
countless caves and mountain roads,
long-standing towns and villages
beyond ordinary unfold.

Grey bubbling mud volcanoes,
waterfalls, hot springs, salt mines,
gold in the belly of mountains
are wonders beyond the divine.

Hills bloom with green pastures
where cattle and sheep graze;
tall haystacks and wild flowers;
crops of wheat, sunflower, maize.

Storks on electricity poles
nest and overlook villagers' lives;
they bring babies in folk tales,
their wide wings brush the skies.

From the north to Black Sea shores,
slow-moving across a vast country
are red and blue trains that crawl
with lowering windows, nonchalantly.

A dreamy air floats and surges
through towns with red-tiled roofs,

wide squares, orthodox churches,
long carpets of cobbled streets.

The Endless Column sky rises
to remember war heroes' triumphs,
whereby Merry Cemetery surprises
with humorous poetic epitaphs.

Margarita Vanyova Dimitrova
BULGARIA

Margarita graduated in Bulgarian philology and German language, and works as a teacher of Bulgarian and German language and literature. She has been published in a number books and publications including *Touch the Milky Way with a smile and hope, Kulski Poetic Fair,* and *Steps 10: Poetry by Bulgarian scientists*, and participates with other teachers and parents in organizing cultural and social activities for young people.
E: margovd@abv.bg

IDENTITY

Deep quietness
      and quiet saintliness
in the space of my favourite birthplace.
From the town of Kula my long way is starting,
uneven,
     inspired
        and
            rediscovering,
Fulfilling the heart with fiery orbs.
It has found the meaning in simple thoughts
    with the breath of the past,
            flowers and sacred trees.
In the traditional dances and the smiles of the people,
in the caress of a sunny day,
in the touch of wisdom with science
     is born my verse inspired.

Syed Ahrar Ali
PAKISTAN

Syed Ahrar was born into a family of poets. With multiple Urdu and Persian language poets in the family, it was only a matter of time before he took up that mantle as well; he found his love for poetry in 2013, when he was introduced to his high school poetry books. Currently he is a writer in an organization, and online for various digital marketing platforms.
E:ahrarali610@gmail.com
FB: @ahrarali2009
Instagram: @ahrarali13

BONDAGE

Him
I tend to stay quiet,
Not saying a word,
But my heart's a riot,
Defiant of the herd.

Her
Your heart's a riot,
I understand it so,
But my mind's disquiet,
For what is below.

Him
I want to go out there,
Finding myself a foe,
I am in the know; aware,
What they will upon me bestow.

Her
You are afraid of unknown,
Fearing what they will bestow,
Yet I roam all alone,
Facing the eyes that glow.

Him
You say the eyes glow,
But what do they show?
Pride, hate or some foe?
I am stuck in a row.

Her
You act as if you don't know,
Nor pride; neither hate they show,
The eyes lustful of the bod,
Circling the prey; the crows.

Him
I say I don't talk,
Walking as an oblivious,
Not knowing the gawks,
They show like lascivious.

Her
That is what I say is wrong,
With the society as whole,
With those who do nothing,
And think they are in control.

Him
I tend to stay quiet,
Not saying a word,
But saying isn't speaking,
I speak with my words.

Her
There are methods to be heard,
If one knows to listen,
But the problem is the herd,
They have formed a garrison.

Him
Then break the chain,
Side by side, as equals
So it doesn't happen again,
Fighting so there ain't a sequel.

Eduard Harents
ALBANIA

Eduard graduated from Yerevan State University, the faculty of Oriental Studies, and Cairo University's Centre of Arabic Language and Culture. He is an author of 10 poetry collections, and has been published in a large number of both Armenian and foreign periodicals and anthologies. Eduard is the most translated Armenian writer of all time, with his work being translated into more than 50 languages. In 2007, 2009, 2011 and 2013, he was awarded in the Best Poetical Series and Best Translation nominations, and 2013, the young poets first prize for the book *Lethargic Vigilance*. Awards also include: The International Literary Prize For Poetry 2015 and 2019, and the Panorama International Literature Award 2020 (India-Italy). In 2016, his book *The life lives me* was published in Belgium, and in 2017, his book *Lethargic Vigilance* was published in Spain. In 2014 he participated in the Festivalul de Internaţionale "Nopţile de Poezie de la Curtea de Argeş" (Romania) and in the Festival Internazionale di Poesia di Genova (Italy).
E: edharents@gmail.com
FB: @Eduard-Harents

Բանաստեղծությունն այս,

որ ինձ հայր է կոչում,

որի աչքերն անծի՛ր ծիծաղներով լիքն են,

իմ տխրության պահին

դողանչո՛ւմ է այնպես,

կարծես իմ ժպիտը

իր կորցրած խաղալի՛քն է...

Բոլոր խաղերում հաղթում է միշտ,

պատմում է իր սիրած աղջիկների մասին,

իսկ քնելուց առաջ

իրամայում է,

որ ես հաֆիաբնե՛րը պատմեմ

                    իմ մանկության ...

Ու ես գնդա՛ծ աշնան նման

փո՛ւլ եմ գալիս իրաշֆիս դեմ ...

Ու զավակիս նիշերն առած ափերիս մեջ՝

ցշնչում եմ.

— Հեֆիա՛րը հենց Դ՛ու ես, խենթո՛ւկ: —

... Եվ այն իրնեվանեից,

որ ես ոչ մի կերպ

                    հեֆիաբ չե՛մ հիշում,

նա խնդմնդո՛ւմ է վրաս

                    ողջ գիշեր՝

                         մինչև լուսաբաց...

Հետո —

կոպերի արանքում պահած զնցոզը խինդի՝

              նեռս է մտնում նինջի խորան:

Թե՞ բնո՛ւմ է երգս,— միայն աչերը բա՛ց ...

42

UNTITLED
Translated from Armenian by Herminée Arshakyan

This poem,
which calls me father,
which eyes are full of endless laughters,
it chimes so in my moments of sadness,
like my smile
is it's lost toy ...
It always wins in every play,
is telling about it's beloved girls,
and before sleeping
he orders,
me to tell the tales of
my childhood ...
And me like a foolish autumn
crumble before my miracle ...
And taken the yells of my child in my palms
I am whispering:
– You self are the fairytale dotty –
... And of the delight,
that I can't remember
any fairy-tale in no way,
he is laughing at me
all the night -
till dawn ...
Then -
the mirth jingle kept between eyelids -
enters to a nap tabernacle.
If my song is sleeping - only with open eyes ...

Krishna Kumar Srinivasan
INDIA

Krishna has been writing poems since he was ten years old and has compiled a collection of poems spanning 50 decades, which he intends to publish in 2022. His work has been published in various print including International media, and he has been awarded in 2002 for his poem on the 9/11 terrorist attack on the World Trade Centre in the USA. His poems touch the very fabric of India and its consciousness, and on his collective experiences in the Middle East, where he worked for over 30 years. His ability to touch upon the nuances of the commonplace, the mundane and the current happenings in the society, form the heart of his poems. He believes in giving voice to his interpretations with well-crafted words that strike a chord with the readers.

E: krsnarti@gmail.com

75 - 15TH AUGUST 2021
(Written on the 75th Indian Independence Day)

I stand with my chin up, proud, and tall
And always at your beck and call
Are you at mine?
While you shine?

I lay my chest bare so you can feed
From my breasts whenever you need
Do you think?
Or even blink?

I watch in utter silence while you fight
Enemies, within and out, with all your might
But fighting each other
Doesn't it you bother?

I choke on my own tears with a muted yell
And see my children starve for a morsel
While many waste
In bad taste

I reel in pain while farmers die hungry
in the fields where they grow rice plenty
Do you hear their screams?
In your lovely dreams?

I am 75 and I have visions dipped in love
For all of you as we are in it hand and glove
Will you make it happen?
Will you listen?

I want you to breathe clean air that blows
From the seas, Himalayas, peaks & lows
Make a promise to work together
And stop blaming each other
Remember forever, I am not just for you
I am here for all your next generations too
I give you, so that you may share
With the needy and poor and care

I am India. I am who you celebrate today
I am the symbol of your Independence Day

MIGRANTS

A few thousand miles into the sky
Soaring cranes crane their neck
Away from wintry white icy wind
Leaving behind their Siberian home

Migrant birds wink at the smiling Indian sun

Pink stained royal flamingos fly
Training their eyes for a water-check
A burst of breeding beaks unwind
As the blushing desert sands bloom

Soaring gently with the soaring Indian sun

Bluethroats, redshanks and herons
Travel like seasoned frequent flyers
Rosy pelicans wander in abrupt freedom
Nocturnal feathers spread unafraid

Poking their way into the rising Indian sun

Somewhere they left the city like felons
They were the society's marginal outliers
Man, child, woman all slaves of a fiefdom
Their dark worker life hit by a surprise raid

Migrants lost into the setting Indian sun

AUTHOR'S NOTE
Due to the Pandemic, thousands of labourers, who were migrant workers coming from other states in India, lost their jobs, and were suffering. The Government failed to help them, and they had to walk several hundred kilometres to get back home to safety. This poem is in honour of these Migrant workers.

Ndue Ukaj
KOSOVO

Ndue is a writer, essayist, poet and literary critic. To date, he has published four poetry books, one short story, and two literary critics. He won several awards, including the National award for best book of poetry published in 2010 in Kosovo. His works have been published in distinguished international anthologies and journals, and have been translated into many languages.
E: ndue.ukaj@gmail.com

SMOKE
Translated by Edita Kuçi Ukaj

It is morning
and the good news doesn't come as the melody of the birds:
it was once a time the spring,
the hope and the awareness that freedom is the absence of slavery.

Now there is smoke and a bad smell
and spring resembles autumn.

Grief waves over our heads
this mortal flag that as a cortège of sadness
spruce from hand to hand.

The good news is not like dreams.
They are written in the tunnels where there is a lack of light,
where darkness powerfully extends the power
on the guards of fate -
those people who play in the theatre of democracy.

The city sleeps restlessly
wakes up agitated
cries and laughs agitated.

Coffees are full of ghosts
and the rumble of bad news.

There is smoke and a flag of grief
which is stretched out like a scarf of pain
on the aggravated neck of a people
that seeks to burst with sadness.

And I took with me a bag of dreams
and I went out into the streets without hope.
I saw people turned into shadows,
a palace of solitude with refreshing props
and with the inscription:
"Freedom is a great deception."

On the way, I kicked stones of thrown grief.
"How much madness carries my city on its shoulders" -
said the girl with the beautiful scarf around her sweet neck
and a black bag of sadness she carried with her.

THE GATEWAY OF FREEDOM
Translated by Edita Kuçi Ukaj

She wakes up with her white nightdress
and her mind flies wherever meaning dwells.
On the first train, she browses the newspaper
which she gets for free,
And get for free what she doesn't need.
Her astonished friend says:
"The gateway of freedom have doors of steel
And the keys are guarded by thugs and robbers."
Her despair grows like clouds on a December day over the Adriatic
Sea.

There is no clarity or clearness anywhere.
Suddenly a stain has spread on her heart
and quickly close the newspaper and truly ask: is freedom with
narrow gateway?

The train informs the next station where she should not stop.
The other goal awaits her - the endless goal she never attains.
Then she sighs and says: the train is not obstructed by fog.
The train meanders with its fury
and fills nature with what it lacks: noise.

Her doubt has no owner.
It is a flood of badly written news
for hers time.

There are elections in her country in the evening.
She reads Hamlet aloud, hears the sounds of upset birds,
and sees the crepes of the clock move furiously against the waiting
wall.

She wakes up next day same with the white nightdress.
It's the day of democracy - the news says,
but the gateway of freedom are closed
and the keys are in the hands of those who possess you,
my freedom -
squeal surprisingly
and waits to stop at the forgotten station.

ALWAYS SOMETHING HAPPENS
Translated by Edita Kuçi Ukaj

It always happens to see a dream and to dream something else.
To be enchanted by one icon and to dream of another icon.
Random to be somewhere and think of another place.
For example,
to be in Rome and suddenly understand
that not all paths lead to happiness.

Or to be in Pristina and to dream of a far place
where freedom has no political smell.
Or being in a far place
and to dream of Pristina with the political smell.

It always happens to come up with ideas and shape the pyramid of words
with beautiful labyrinths and magnificent icons.

It always happen to accomplish something and search for something else;
to be with someone and look for someone else.

It always happens to look for the pyramid of happiness
and to be overturned in the triangle of sorrow,
whose boundary happens to be invisible
where you get confused like a drunkard who does not keep his balance
and sees people lined upholding white papers
in their black hands.

They look at the blue sky
and out of their pockets, they draw poems that become readable
just when there is sunlight.
In an evening when the magical time is shaped for you and me.

A PAPER
Translated by Edita Kuçi Ukaj

A paper may be more important
that the weight of your desires,
of dreams
of all the pain you carry in your chest,
on heavy shoulders;
more than blue eyes where ships of desire enter and go out
more than a heart attacked by storms and tsunamis.

It can increase the pain or reduce it.

A paper can define:
where you can go and where not,
a letter called a permit to cross the border,
where the laws of passage there depend on someone,
as they are dependent here on someone else.

Human life is full of boundaries, obstacles, temptations,
sadly a letter can reduce your body weight,
the severity of the pain
of love,
of desires,
of dreams,
of sadness,
a letter can reduce the amount of joy,
the amount of happiness.
A letter can measure the amount of breathing,
oxygen in the body, tension, pulse.
Because we are always surrounded by borders
that appears and disappears quite suddenly in our lives.

We know that borders have control,
police and soldiers ready with weapons in hand to carry out orders,
but we never do the right thing to replace them
with clover flowers,
beautiful sculptures and spring dreams.

Because the real boundaries are in the language,
in morning dreams and bad desires of night.

Astonishingly, people do not like borders,
but they are not used to live without them,
therefore they seldom understand the weight of a letter
that determines how much you weigh,

who are you
and can you go where ever you want.

Boundaries are a burden and people are doomed to suffer
within them,
therefore they find it difficult to increase the size of the heart,
of language,
of soul,
of dreams
and create the magnificent kingdom of love.

Rana Zaman
BANGLADESH

Md. Shamsuzzaman Bhuiyan, aka Rana Zaman, retired as an Additional Secretary to the Government of Bangladesh in February 2019. His first poetry book was published in 1999. He has since had over 90 poems, short stories and rhymes published in books, magazines and online platforms around the world.
E: rana2344@gmail.com

A VILLAGE CALLED UJANI

The gentle effluxing river flows through
the ribs of the village
Increasing the beauty crowding of stars
has increased around the village
Lying on the river bank sailing boats are floating
Ships moved effortlessly holding the sound to its chest

Listening the charming song of boatman
village-made open door at night
The mind become crazy hearing the enchanting
melody of the shepherd's flute
Hearing the guard's whistle, hiding in the cave
the fox cry in failure
Foolish thieves are caught in the trap of all dogs

In winter, the village-maid goes to fetch
water soaking her feet in the grass
Everyone eats the honey of the new hive by sharing
Cow-carts on dirt roads and mechanical vehicles
ply on paved roads
See-saw dances in somebody's house,
someone husk paddy in machine
Some work in the village factory, some run the plough
Everyone has a self-sufficient forest with their house
If any crime happens then an excellent settlement
is made in arbitration
They opened a grocery store as there is no work for police

Politicians have no place in that village
If someone enters by mistake, he has to climb the tree quickly

When spring comes, the cuckoo calls in a sweet tone
After eating bananas monkeys does not leave peel here

The villagers catch fish in the village Ujani in a group
No one's ears are ever being snatched by an invisible kite
They drink tube well water; the water of the pond is also good
No one in Ujani village remembers the slightest sorrow.

Mandy Macdonald
SCOTLAND

Originally from New South Wales, Australia, Mandy is a writer, translator and editor who came to Britain as a student in the late 1960s, and seems not to have gone home yet, except for rare visits. She has also lived and worked in Cuba and Central America, and has written widely on that region. Mandy has been writing poems for most of her life, but only started sharing them after taking part in Jo Bell's inspiring '52' project in 2014/15. She is now a Pushcart Prize nominee, and has had over 250 poems published in anthologies and magazines including *Causeway/Cabhsair, Poetry Scotland*, and *A Christmas Canzonette*. Her first collection *The temperature of blue* was published in 2020 (Blue Salt Collective). Recently she has made poems about the advancing climate catastrophe, some of which appear in *Earth Days Numbered* and *Counting Down the Days* (published in late 2021 by Grey Hen Press in support of the UK Youth Climate Coalition), *Rebel Talk* (Extinction Rebellion Oxford, 2021), and *Words from the Brink*, (Arachne Press, Solstice Shorts 2021). Her performance piece *Requiem* for a sunburnt country, a response to the bushfires that devastated much of Australia in late 2019 and early 2020, was staged in Canberra at a large choral concert, 'New Life, New Hope', in March 2020. She is currently working towards a new small collection and deepening her knowledge of haiku and other small Japanese-inspired forms. She hopes that music and poetry will help her survive the near future, but is cultivating an allotment just in case.

E: mandy.macdonald@gmail.com

THE HOLY NAMES OF MARY

Could I have been anything but Mary?
Every Catholic girl was Mary something:
my mother, Mary Margaret;
her grandmother, Mary Sophia.

Dolores, Socorro, Pilar, Tránsito – born in Spain,
I might have been
Mary of the Seven Dolours
        Mary of Perpetual Succour
                Mary the Pillar
                        Mary of the Transit, even.

Having defaulted to the name of the Virgin, however,
my parents lost interest. At the very last minute –
by earthly law – Daddy was dispatched
down to the registry office
to tag something on to that mandatory Mary.
Anything you like, my mother said, milky
and slovenly with sleeplessness. So he chose
Anne.

Within months even she had given up on it,
begun calling me Miranda.

EARLY MORNING ON ST PATRICK'S DAY, SYDNEY

All around the Harbour, regeneration rules:
curated, honey-coloured foreshores
sand-blasted out of local stone,
native trees planted in elegant tableaux.
Immaculate, the land's edge mimics what it was
before whitefellas ever limped ashore, half-dead
from hungry months at sea, straw-bedded on hard ballast.

***

Almost a tourist now, after so long an absence,
I walk this artful shoreline. Still, that drop of Ireland
courses in my blood, the gift of my great-grandmother,
whose name I have. What hunger, shame, ambition
drove her here, a century and a half ago,
from that County Mayo village – Ballinrobe, was it?
Or Knock, it might have been, or some other – no one
really seemed to know, or to welcome the telling, and
they are all gone now.
                              Somehow
she fetched up in Araluen, the Dreamtime Vale
of Waterlilies, among a brawl of miners;
stayed, married, mothered, would have seen
that valley befouled and scoured
in the wild scramble for gold.

It was said in the family she had arrived with nothing
but a trunk full of books. A teacher, like her daughter
 and her granddaughter, my mother? Or overseer
to a shipload of orphan girls scooped up
from famine-glutted workhouses, shipped away
to serve as maids and cooks and wives?

***

There will be High Mass today
at old St Patrick's of the Rocks, and lesser sacrifices
citywide – boxty, Guinness, Old Bushmill's –
offered by the descendants of those starvelings
who gulped back their horrified dismay
at sight of Port Jackson's gaunt contorted shore,
crossed themselves for grace,

rolled up their sleeves, kilted their filthy skirts
and set about building a new Ireland.

Xe M. Sánchez
SPAIN

Xe was born in 1970 in Grau (Asturies, Spain). He received his Ph.D in History from the University of Oviedo in 2016, he is anthropologist, and he also studied Tourism, and has three masters. He has published in Asturian language *Escorzobeyos* (2002), *Les fueyes tresmanaes d'Enol Xivares* (2003), *Toponimia de la parroquia de Sobrefoz. Ponga* (2006), *Llué, esi mundu paralelu* (2007), *Les Erbíes del Diañu* (E-book: 2013, Paperback: 2015), *Cróniques de la Gandaya* (E-book, 2013), *El Cuadernu Prietu* (2015), and several publications in journals and reviews in Asturies, USA, Portugal, France, Sweden, Scotland, Australia, South Africa, India, Italy, England, Canada, Reunion Island, China, Belgium, Ireland and the Netherlands.
E: sanchez.xe.m@gmail.com

TWO AT LEAST

all of us preserve (at least)
two cultural identities:
our official identity
(look for it
over the official papers),
and our own real identity
(a hidden treasure
sheltered in our mind,
different in each of us,
that special country
where poetry springs
and where the fountains,
the wood, the mountains,
the sacred spirits
and our particular ghosts
can still remember our name
and the lullabies
singing in our mother tongue).

Monique Holton
AUSTRALIA

Monique s a contributor to *Stereo Stories* and *Poets Corner* at *InReview*. She was a recent category winner of the Spineless Wonders '100 Words of Butterfly' Writing Competition, and an upcoming contributor to *CafeLit*. Monique is currently working on her first young adult novel.
E: monique_holton@hotmail.com
W: www.moniqueholton.com

THE CUL-DE-SAC

The cul-de-sac sat nestled in a maze of streets. Bitumen grids carved freshly into the hillside which once was a paddock. The cows old stomping ground invaded by cookie cutter houses on quarter acre lots. Mum and Dad's very own slice of the great Australian dream. We were the weekend militants. The baby-faced army of the dead-end. An assortment of neighbourhood kids, blue-collar spawn, sent off to battle with a single command, 'take your sister with you'. The steep incline of the road would not be tolerated today. Millennials would expect excavated perfection. But to us it was an asphalt playground. A cascading stream of gravel and tar; a Niagara for bikes and scooters and skates. Bianka was there. The new girl with the strange accent and European tan, winning us over with her mum's thin ginger biscuits. Accepted into our troupe of freckles and scabs and grazes. In the distance, the dads take the emerald stage for an eighteen-hole production. A round of applause the clap of polished wood against white dimpled ball. Whilst the mums own performance is underway, a dance of housework tango, the Hoover taking the lead in the living room theatre. Our playtime dismissal was signalled by the sunset. The peach skied timer ringing us home and met appreciatively with dinner of meat and three veg. Dad's strap draped intentionally over the back of his chair, an unspoken warning to eat our greens. Simultaneously, after Daryl and his crew had 'Hey Hey'd' our Saturday, a chorus of running water transcends over the street. Baths are drawn, water is turned grey and the days grime swirls clockwise into the chrome abyss. Skinny weary bodies, little sacks of bone and skin are rested on clouds of synthetic foam where dreams are made of bitumen grids and cul-de-sac mazes.

Jen Ross

ARUBA

Jen is an award-winning Chilean-Canadian journalist and social scientist whose non-fiction stories have been published and/or broadcast in hundreds of media around the world. Born in Ottawa, Canada—to a Chilean mother and Canadian father—she was raised in a multicultural environment, travelled to more than 50 countries and has lived in five. She speaks six languages and holds a Bachelor of Journalism with a minor in Anthropology from Carleton University, a Master of Arts in Political Studies from Queen's University, and a Master of Science in International Relations from the London School of Economics and Political Science. Jen has more than 20 years of professional writing, editing and strategic communications experience in media and with the United Nations—including the Economic Commission for Latin America and the Caribbean, UN Human Rights and UN Women. In 2016, she took a leave of absence and moved to her husband's island, Aruba, where she wrote her first fiction and poetry. Her debut short story collection was longlisted for the Mslexia Novel Competition 2017. She decided to stay in paradise, where she now works as a university lecturer and editorial consultant.
E: jen.reporter@gmail.com
W: www.jen-ross.com

MIXED BLOODS

We are a mosaic of cultures and sacrifices.
A woven tapestry of silk and ashes.
The blood of four continents runs through our veins
Europe, Asia, North and South America – with question marks in
between.

That blue patch on our lower back has faded
along with our childhood, our innocence,
our memories of lands conquered and betrayed,
and names changed to hide our religion.

We are the conquerors and the conquered,
talking of retribution while holding the latest iphone.
Our dreams of justice and equality dashed,
then reignited every other generation.

Six languages roll off our tongues,
Our skin tinted by more than one race.
We are multi-ethnic, multicultural, mixed bloods. Shades of grey.
Some call us half-breeds, but is there such thing as a quarter breed?

We are Catholic, Protestant, Buddhist, Jewish and spiritual
A collision of cultures and beliefs.
But what is culture, really?
Our lives have been steeped in tradition, festivals, music … and
expectations.

Boats and airplanes bring tears to our eyes
with the promise of new adventures,
or the comfort and the safety of home.
But which home? There are so many...

Where are you from? How to answer that question?
when you love all people and you don't know what you are.
Is 'culturally nonbinary' a thing?
We are one global family. One humanity.

Our identity is a mangled knot of blood, beliefs and memories of
where we've been.
We are melancholy for the past.
We are happy. We are angry. We are often dysfunctional.
But we know we are loved.

A SENSE OF HOME

The sights
of crystalline snowflakes glinting off the fresh snowbanks in the morning,
of salmon sunsets splashed against the backdrop of the snow-capped Andes,
of clear turquoise blue waters lapping against ivory shores.

The scents
of damp earth after a torrential downpour and the thaw after a long winter,
of gnarled knots of cochayuyo drying in the sun on misty mornings by the sea,
of fresh keri keri stewing and fried funchi served in a wicker basket.

The tastes
of beavertails, hot cocoa and maple syrup hardened on fresh snow,
of sweet manjar, Lucy's potato tortillas and just-baked empanadas,
of fresh figs and Antillean papayas from my mother-in-law's garden.

The sounds
of Maestro Fresh Wes at school dances and Sarah McLachlan CDs after a break-up,
of Juan Luis Guerra on New Year's Eve and of reed flutes echoing across the Andes,
of the Trade winds blowing while trupials and chuchubis chirp their morning songs.

The touch
of tall grasses and ripe dandelion heads blowing into my hair,
of abuelita's soft wrinkled arms embracing us before we leave, again,
of tight hugs and cheeks brushing one after another at extended-family gatherings.

I have lived in many countries but there are three I can call home.
They linger in my soul, in my body, and in my memories,
Fragments of a nomadic life filled with love, longing, insecurity and adventure.

THE INVISIBLE MINORITY

Looking puzzled, they stare
at my white skin, and declare:
You're not Latina.
Until my perfect Spanish dispels their doubts.

Then they meet someone with copper skin and ask where they're from:
Canada? What about your parents? ... Canada. And your grandparents?,
fishing for whatever 'other' it is they're looking for.
They'll consider them more authentic—more ethnic—than me.

The conflict between race and ethnicity
can confound and confuse one's identity.
When your skin colour doesn't match people's assumptions,
it breeds an alienation and extraction from one's roots.

Yet in Latin America, culture transcends colour.
We are white, black, copper and all shades in between.
With traits that are Indigenous, Caucasian, African and/or Asian.
I'm not light or dark enough to be seen as a foreigner in Chile.

But despite the colour of my skin,
I have experienced racism in Canada.
When I couldn't speak English, my teacher called me dumb.
When I wore clothes abuelita made, my classmates mocked me.

Here, in my land of snow and of many immigrants,
Minorities can be invisible too.
Maybe one day they'll forget their preconceived notions
and see us for who we are, not where we're from.

Jonathan Ukah
ENGLAND

Jonathan is a graduate of English from the University of Nigeria. He studied Law in Germany, but lives and writes in London, UK.
E: johnking1502@gmail.com

WHEN WE DECIDE TO HAVE A COUNTRY

And when we decide to have a country,
Will it be forged of our incarcerated bodies
Like piled-up pieces of wood on a pyre?
Will it be born of the dark and orange sun,
Soaked up in the blood of the angry,
Who died in vain, their hearts torn;
Between dismal, sunless grimace
Through sacrifices of flesh and blood,
Self-denial, long years of tortuous race
Incarceration of our spirit and spotting blood.
Or will be like a forest of sublime quiet,
Wild animals gazing with wonder in their eyes
As preys limp to their destined places of rest.

Previously published by *The Sparrows Trombone* (October 2021).

THE TRAVELLER

I travelled around the world
In search of beauty,
I did not carry it with me,
and I found it not.

Like the hummingbird
Hopping from tree to tree
In search of the best fruit
That nature could ever have.

I saw nations sleep in squalor
As flags wave with rugged arms
Leaders shouting in parliaments
It is topsy-turvy everywhere.

The home shall be a blessing
The children surround the table,
But I saw fathers kiss the mothers
Drawing streams of blood

I met with the richest governments,
Walked in tapestries of gold,
Soldiers marched behind me
With platoons of armoured cars.

I saw kings and princes in palaces,
Gold and ornaments are strewn around,
But I heard shrill cries of pain,
From children abandoned by mothers.

Cities splash with envious wealth,
Kingdoms dancing in diamonds,
Sequinned scents spewed everywhere,
Sewers are strewn with dreadful dirt.

I met the poor and the wretched,
The creams of wealth and power,
But I heard moans of mothers
Tearful lamentations at midnight.

The sun shone on the rich and poor,
The rain hit them both,

The tempest and the sultry storm
There is no peace everywhere.

I travelled around the world indeed,
Searching for a modicum of beauty,
But I did not carry it with me,
Sadly I found it not.

Ali Alhazmi
SAUDI ARABIA

Born in Damadd, Saudi Arabia, Ali obtained a degree in Arabic Language and Literature at Umm Al-Qura University, Faculty of Arabic Language. As early as 1985, Ali started publishing his poetry in a variety of local and Arabic international cultural publications including *The Seventh Day* (Paris), *Creativity* (Cairo), *Nazoa* (Amman) and *The New Text*. He has participated various International Poetry Festivals including; Costa Rica (2013), Spain (2014), Uruguay (2015), Cuba, Colombia and Turkey (2016), Italy and Romania (2017) and Spain (2018). His work has been translated into many languages, and his publications include: *A Gate for the Body* (1993), *Loss* (2000), *Deer Drink Its Own Image* (2004), *Comfortable on the Edge* (2009), and *Now in the Past* (2018). His awards include: Medal of Poetry (Uruguay, 2015), The World Grand Prize for Poetry, (Romania 2017), the Verbumlandi Prize (Italy, 2017) and Best International Poet (China, 2018).
E: ali-alhazmi@hotmail.com
FB: @Alhazmi.ali

THROWING YOUR GRIEF AS A ROCK INTO THE SEA

In your forties,
Wingless,
You urge the meaning to fly once again,
As though you are powerful enough, once more, To step over the clouds.
Heading towards your own wilderness,
The winds put all sins of the tale upon your shoulders. Since you stopped at the gates of your past,
With chained legs,
Neither your years returned to the song,
Nor did the gorgeous girls come back
From the trees of childhood jocundly
To your fields.

In your forties,
There, near the springs,
Longing takes you towards the deer,
That no more listen to your songs,
When you feel their approaching foot-steps, And when the bird of words chirps
On a lonely branch in the heart.
You throw your grief like a rock into the sea. And see your face burning
In the furnace of the lost painful moment.

In your forties,
When you are fastened
To the flutes on the shawl of a ballad,
Find a dove forgotten in your own travelling meaning. Do not exhaust the tender melody
With sighs of the memory that circle around your soul like a bracelet.

In your forties,
The past assumes you are so close to its orchards,
While you are there still stuck in the wilderness of your fantasies.
When you started your voyage
Towards your glittering metaphor,
You paid no attention to the thorny questions
Staring from afar at your feet.

In your forties on the roads,
No more you need to fold your shadows, as you head towards the

pleasures of life, trying to reach the lost bank of the river.

Memory asks, "When was it when you went bewildered In the presence of oblivion?"
What would have hurt your innocent past if you stopped at its noble gates for greeting,
For dropping off the burdens of rejection
that have watered your eyes with thirst of nothingness?"

In your forties,
A woman from the past visits you;
Don't be rude to her flutes
By asking about her distant love stories. Save her from the deceptive mills. Restore her to pure joy,
and to her flowers.
Listen to the bird of her soul
neglected in the trees of absence.
Be like soft rains for her if she goes astray. Be a metaphorical chord if she smiles. And be an existential passion,
if she looks at you.

But, when you approach her extensive fires, Be nothing but ashes.

Monsif Beroual
MOROCCO

Monsif is a multi-awarded and internationally renowned poet. He graduated in Public Law in Arabic from Sidi Mohammed Ben Adlalah University, Taza City, and holds his Master Degree in Strategic Studies and Decision Making. His poems have been translated into Spanish, French, Chinese, Polish, Arabic, Romanian, Bulgarian, Serbian, Croatian, Italian and Taiwanese, and published in more than 300 international anthologies and magazines.
E: monsifberoual@yahoo.com
FB: @Monsif Beroual

MOROCCO SEED

The real history that I love
Between human lives
A brother, a sister
No matter which colour that we belong to
Oldest streets will speak out about this united love
Temple, church, mosque, together in love
Ask our brothers Jewish about Morocco lands
That I really appreciate as a human in this land
Morocco seed, that makes me feel my root
As a human being
Under the sky of love
And lands of humane heart

Brian Langley
AUSTRALIA

Brian lives in suburban Perth, the capital of Western Australia with his wife of fifty plus years. His poetry has changed direction somewhat, now being mostly classified as Australian Bush Poetry; rhyming poetry which has near perfect metre and consistency of structure. He writes across many subjects and performs (mostly from memory) regularly at retirement villages, aged care facilities, country festivals, service and social clubs etc., etc., under the name The City Poet - this is due to him being a member of the Western Australian Bush Poets Association, many members of which have a rural background and write on rural subjects - most of his poetry is from the point of view of an Australian city dweller. His poems reflect his lifestyle, age and interests, mainly ageing, being Australian, the environment, travelling, fishing and contemporary living. He also delves occasionally into politics and history. He has self-published several books, as well as some audio CDs, and a couple of e-books of historic Western Australian poetry.
E: briandot@tpg.com.au
W: www.Brianlangley.wabushpoets.asn.au

I'M PROUD TO BE AUSTRALIAN

I'm proud to be Australian
I wear the Aussie gear
I wear it on Australia Day
And sometimes through the year

The hat, the vest, the rubber thongs
and shorts that show me knees
There's just one little problem
They're all made overseas

As if that isn't bad enough
They also make the toys
Those cuddly Aussie animals
We give to girls and boys

There's Chinese Platypuses
Koalas from Taiwan
Kangaroos from Bangladesh
And wombats from Ceylon

And what about the souvenirs
The ones the traveller buys
Reminders of Australia
The beaches, sun and flies

The tea towels, spoons and postcards
That show the Harbour Bridge
You'd think that they'd be made right here
That they'd be ridgey didge

But no, just like my clothing,
Most other Aussie gear
Is made in places overseas
It should be made right here

It should be true blue, dinkum stuff
There ought to be some laws
That says our Aussie Icons must
Be made here - on our shores.

OUR NATIONAL FOOD

Most countries have foods that their neighbours don't eat,
Germans turn blood into some kind of meat.
Arabs eat sheep's eyes, or so I've been told,
and Chinese eat eggs, a hundred years old.

There's many a country eat chilli so hot,
you really don't know if you're breathing or not.
The French, they eat snails and frog's legs as well.
The English eat eels suspended in gel.

Some people eat monkey and other eat rat.
Eskimo people eat blubber and fat.
The Scots they eat haggis though goodness knows why,
and the Yanks out of pumpkin make some sort of pie.

Now Japanese people eat seaweed with rice.
Some African people think warm blood is nice.
Norwegians are known to eat raw fish as snacks,
and folk from Tibet, they eat butter from yaks.

The folks from these countries I know they'd abhor,
the food of our nation, that we all adore.
For here in Australia, what do we see,
but a product that comes from the Vegemite tree.

Now Vegemite trees, you wont see around,
your neighbourhood garden. They are only found
In a few small locations, top secret they are;
the trees that make Vegemite, thick in its jar.

For the Vegemite comes from the sap of the tree,
collected at night-time when no one can see;
From a slit in the bark, to fill up each jar,
then the slit seals over to a slightly raised scar.

The trees must be tapped in the dark of the night;
if done during daylight it wouldn't be right.
For the sap in the daytime is tasteless and pale,
totally worthless, unsuited for sale.

Each night after sunset, as people retire,
or they sit watching TV, in front of the fire,
The workers assemble; in buses and cars,

they come to attach all the Vegemite jars

To the trees in their hundreds, they use special clips,
and small plastic spouts to direct all the drips
From the cuts that they make in the tree's slippery bark.
The vegemite oozes out there in the dark.

It's a specialised job, there's few in the know;
if the cut is too big, then the jars overflow
And the Vegemite's wasted, it drips to the ground,
just food for the insects when morning comes round.

And what if the cut is too narrow or short?
Not enough Vegemite sap will be caught,
And those jars will be useless and not fit for sale,
with all of the problems that that will entail.

Now, there's just one more thing that each Aussie should know.
The product that comes from the trees that we grow
Is untouched by humans, it's as pure as can be;
it goes straight in the jar from the Vegemite tree.

And so as you raise to the mouth on your head,
some Vegemite smeared upon butter and bread,
And you take a deep breath and delight in the smell:
You just know you're Australian, wherever you dwell.

And should you be travelling in overseas places,
and breakfast with people of different races,
And you fish in your pocket and out comes a jar,
of Vegemite, thick and black just like tar,

And they see what you're eating and ask for a lick,
'tis better than evens, 'twill make them feel sick,
And they'll say in a voice devoid of all wit,
That stuff is so awful, it tastes just like ... (pause)

And they say, in their country, it just wouldn't sell,
but they ask, in their ignorance, please can you tell
Us. - What is it made from, that horrible stuff,
that one tiny taste of, was more than enough.

Don't tell them the truth, of the Vegemite tree,
and the sap that is gathered when no-one can see;
Just spin them a yarn, just tell them you think,
it's the leftover stuff from the beer that we drink.

Bharti Bansal
INDIA

Bharti is a 24 year old poet from Shimla, India. She loves the moon, the universe, cats and poetry. Her works have appeared in *aaduna*, *Harness magazine*, *Oc87recoverydiaries.org* and others.
E: ar.bansal2011@gmail.com
Instagram: @bharti_b42

NAME

"A name, thin as air, can also be a shield." Ocean Vuong

I have always been afraid of taking my name out loud. Because saying it means I am occupying some space in this universe and that scares me. It means I can be heard then, and people can label me as they please. I wonder if we could communicate in sign language, what would my name look like. Maybe I would just point at my face and let people know that I am talking about myself for once. It becomes difficult, to be so small that people start mistaking you for a full stop, putting you where a sentence/relationship ends. It's one thing to be treated as someone's priority and other, to be so ignored that you have to constantly shout out loud about your existence. All my friendships have been only me shouting,screaming. The act of death is the biggest way to memorialise a name, maybe that's why when Ocean Vuong compared it to thin air, he meant names and ghosts can be same sometimes. I am a breath away from becoming a memory yet I choose to take it every single time because perhaps when these lips come together to form Bharti, they mean it as a symbol of love. Maybe saying your name is self love after all. Maybe when two bodies melt together, and whisper speak each other's names, they after all use it to tell that they are going to stay even when these bodies act like shields, separating their beating hearts. But don't you think if fist represents the size of hearts, holding each other's hands is the most intimate way one can say; *"here, take my hand, open this fist gently and know this heart still keeps your name."*

Amelia Fielden
AUSTRALIA

Amelia a writer, poet and translator, who has spent most of her adult life engrossed in Japanese culture; she has lived in the country for extensive periods, and is fluent in the Japanese language. In retirement Amelia has settled in the seaside city of Wollongong in south-eastern Australia.
E: anafielden@gmail.com

RAKED GRAVEL

no other word
but 'dancing' could describe
the progress
through this Zen garden
of a black butterfly

So much of what I love about Japan is here, in the grounds of an old wooden temple.
A hundred metres and several hundred years up the cobbled lane from a major
thoroughfare, such peace.

at noon, empty
of priests and worshippers,
the temple precinct
thrums with the transience
of summer cicadas

My guide today is my dearest Japanese friend, Nariko.
There is the deep understanding of almost half a century in our relationship.
How fortunate I am to sit with her now, sipping green tea under the veranda eaves
as we silently contemplate that dancing butterfly.

Previously published in *Mint Tea From A Copper Pot & other tanka tales*, by Amelia Fielden (Ginninderra Press, 2013).

A TALE OF TWO CAKES

Once upon a time when I was a poor foreign student in Tokyo, I happened to meet at the local railway station a poor Japanese student who was living in the same humble lodgings. Strolling home together we came to a stop before the window of a glamorous patisserie.

"Oh,look," exclaimed Marko, "*mont-blanc* ... of course it's autumn now."

An Australian raised on fruit cake and lamingtons, I had no idea what she was talking about. With a hungry gleam in her eyes, Mariko explained that *mont-blanc* is a type of cup cake, topped with pale brown chestnut puree in the shape of a mountain, and crowned with a whole candied chestnut. Japanese food is very seasonal, and chestnuts are an autumn speciality.

We pooled our yen and bought just one *mont-blanc*. Back in Mariko's tiny tatami-mat room, we shared that cake and a pot of green tea. Delicious!

Two years later, diagnosed with tuberculosis, Mariko left her Piano Academy and returned to Kyushu to die.

sometimes I dream
of that other life, and
Mariko
forever twenty-three
all these years I have lived

Another era, another part of Japan. Not so poor now, I was dining in late spring with a charming university teacher.

On the dessert menu I found the item '*ajisai mont-blanc*','*hydrangea mont-blanc*'.

Curious, I asked for this when my companion ordered our coffees. With a bow the waiter presented to me, on a plate decorated with real hydrangea petals, a classically formed *mont-blanc* cake, whose chestnut puree was coloured the same purple as the flower petals.
 Of course ... May is the season for celebrating hydrangea in Japan.

indulging me
with the exotic cake
I fancied,
he smilingly denied
my stronger desires

he and I
so much in common
so much to say ...
both loving this country,
alas not each other

In the summer of the following year, enjoying an afternoon snack of perennial red bean buns in Kyoto with the editor of a Japanese poetry journal, I recounted to her my *mont-blanc* episodes.
"Ah," she commented, "through those two cakes you, a foreigner to our culture, have truly experienced aware, the pitifully transient nature of life and love."

my life
is what it is, still
contemplating
Japanese tanka
love, longing, and loss

Previously published in *Mint Tea From A Copper Pot & other tanka tales*, by Amelia Fielden (Ginninderra Press, 2013).

David Brady
PORTUGAL / ENGLAND

David is an English language teacher and aspiring poet who is originally from the UK but currently residing in Lisbon. He works with students from all over the world, helping them to access education. His love for poetry began when he ran a creative writing group in college, and wrote and contributed to the college newspaper. His poetry has been published in *Wilderness House Literary Review, Red Lemon Review* and *Alternate Route*. He enjoys exploring themes relating to the human experience, particularly the interplay between tragedy and nature.

E: dbrady84702@hotmail.com
Twitter: @DJBrady

FOREIGNER

Where do their rivers begin?
Like an enchantment, they sing back to me
in another language.

I walk through storms with no rain.
Clouds part to form the lisp of a soft c.
Rs rumble like murmurs, rolling
through rocks like distant thunder.

I imagine the taste of their tongues.
Hear the wordless call of finches.
in search of worms in far-off, nearby lands.

Yes. I must learn the rivers of Iberia.
Trace their routes on the backs of my hands.
Let their sediments exfoliate my skin. Glisten
in a new sun.

FARMHOUSE IN THE PYRENEES

A wealth of memories settles under the gaze
as hay baled into stacks in a thatched barn,
where dried husks from last year's harvest,
not fit for mouths, nourished the ground.
Where everything the eye touched was plowed
from love or soil: the hay meadows where
we lost our childhoods. Places we knew,
even then, we could never return to.
Where farmers earned bread with the
gentle jab of tools. The tops of wheat
toasting in the June air. Now,
the choke and glare of a city,
where life stacks among a
poverty of things.

Jude Brigley
WALES

Jude has been a teacher, an editor and a performance poet, and is now writing more for the page. She has a chapbook, *Labours* (*Thynks*), and has been published in a range of magazines including: *otherwise Engaged*, *Blue Nib*, *Sylvia* and *Scissortail*.
E: judeteach@icloud.com

TAKE-OFF

At sixteen, she takes the long ascent
to the local cemetery, high
on the hill's side and searches out

the dead: the forebears and forerunners.
She knows them through stories and the great
Grandpa whose room is now hers. Being

fanciful she speaks to the dead
of her blue-prints, never
considering that those at home will

one day also lie abed. Instead, she
listens to the wind stir the grasses
and steals a flower as tribute,

apologising to the sleeping stranger.
On the descent, the streets
seem grey, the hills, though doused in

sunshine, fuse her wings.
Yet, she flies through the familiar lane,
feeling a bridled energy assert itself,

as if life is revving to begin.
Instead, of bustling home, she squats
upon the jutting heap where blue

ironwork slag sparkles like frozen
sea and views the town,
as prison, prism, map and penitentiary,

like some mini Tereshkova,
oblivious to what distant prospect
she longs to make her story.

And in the twilight, she sees her dead
who toiled in ironworks and mine
pointing to the launch of the mind's flight.

DETOUR

She avoided the route through main street,
choosing to take backroads, rather than view

the shop awnings or the jolly summer flags
tossed against blue skies. Their celebratory

waving was in contrast to boarded up buildings.
 She did not want to see Leslie's Store, now

dilapidated where once Santa handed her chalk
and slate in clear prediction of her future career.

 She did not want her mother's voice calling out
in her head, 'Hello beautiful old Bedford Falls'

as if to charm the crumbling Edwardian streets
into a mythic past. Instead, she took the bottom

road past terraces and the Regal Cinema now
transformed into a place of worship. It was a gesture,

a defiant finger at memory's attempt to squeeze
with her melancholic and equivocal grip.

INVESTIGATIONS

If on Google Earth, you search Plasnewydd Street
and get that little figure icon to stand out on the road,
it will appear as if you are at my mother's front door.

But this is spooky It is not 2021 anymore and the house
seems still occupied as my parents' blue car waits
attendance on them. In the parlour window- geraniums

and a plant with white buds I cannot name but recognise.
If only I could turn the handle and go in, my mother
would be sat at the kitchen table with her crossword, a tin

of coke open and a glass half full. It appears as if we are
zooming down way back but really the street is frozen.
It is an illusion that makes us feel we could step inside.

Always intrigued by time, only in writing can I fire
up the machine which returns to my beginnings.
Stories say that to meet your old self on your journey

would bring some dismal catastrophic destiny
but I would risk it for one chance to re-meet those
who carved out my identity and left their traces.

Fahredin Shehu
KOSOVO

Fahredin is a poet, writer, essayist and Independent Scientific Researcher in the field of World Spiritual Heritage and Sacral Aesthetics. Passionate about poetry, painting and calligraphy, Fahredin has participated in many festivals and conferences including the International Poetry Festival Voix de la Mediterranee, the Struga Poetry Events, the Nisan Poetry Festival, the PEN Macedonia 50th anniversary, the Malta Literary Festival, the Maelstrom Poetry Festival, the Sapanca Literary Festival and many others. His poetry is translated in English, German, French, Italian, Spanish, Greek, Polish, Serbian, Croatian, Bosnian, Macedonian, Roma, Swedish, Turkish, Persian, Arabic, Hebrew, Romanian, Chinese/Mandarin, Bahasa, Bengali, Maltese, Frisian and Sicilian, and has been published in several international literary magazines and anthologies including *The World Poets Yearbook 2009, Poetas del Mundo, Blue Max Magazine, Tribune de Geneve, Check Point Poetry, Le Reti di Dedalus, Alquimia de la Terra, Ann Arbor Review, Coldnoon Literary Magazine, World Healing World Peace Anthology, Anthology for the Rights of Hazara People* and many others. He has published over 20 books, and was honoured as the Poet Laureate - Gold Medal for Poetry as a Bridge to Nations. He is also the recipient of Naji Naaman Literary Prize for Poetry in 2016, the Veilero Prize for Poetry in 2017, and nominated for the Pulitzer Prize in 2018. He is the Director and Organizer of International Poetry Festival Poetry and Wine, in Kosovo, and was awarded with Doctor Honoris Causa, Presidential Medal and Lifetime Academic by the Universum Academy, Switzerland.
E: fahredin.shehu@gmail.com
W: www.fekt.org
FB: @Fahredin-Shehu-341712843557

THE WORDS WRITTEN ON THE TAPESTRY OF TIME

When your mind is just as balloon
floating in the wind and
the words of Nowness
scattered on the Tapestry of Time
get the ageless Gitta and
unfold the secret of the strength
learn to debate your doubts and
learn to read yourself
within the chest of the Time
so may it be ...!

And when the stubborn and
invisible dust among page-leaves
makes your nib heavy and
the tongue is knotted and
the sole utterance of the vibe
makes your heart heavy
get the eternal Love out of
which the wordless speech disperse throughout Time and
unfold the secret of the vision
to see every bit of yourself around and
every bit of everything
within yourself and
learn to understand
the differences of the outside
to the same-ness of the inside
so be it ...!

THE TAPESTRY OF DREAMS

That blue vastness ...
I still remember the breeze
that blew dry golden grape leaves
so gently and the Aldehydes and
Oceanic smell as if Oakmoss
is added to strengthen and fixate
that splendid fragrance

What a Time it was?
What a remembrance of
a deluded youth, enthusiastic
to conquer by his will
the entire dimension while
this small blue Planet
was so narrow
was so common and mere to him

Even the tastes were different
the apricots, peaches of the valley
and honey melons in the summer
quinces, nuts, chestnuts and,
pumpkins preserved for winters
very icy cold Balkan winters
when it cracked my lips and
froze the wetness on my eyelashes
and the breath condensing on
the wool shawl made by
my Mother

THE SALT OF AGES

She sat under the shade of the blue wisterias for who knows how many
Man-years waiting an old Soul in the body of an orphan who run away from the sunlight and avoids the rain in August.

He has the azure eyes that shows the emptiness inside yet the heart is full of ruby crystals as pomegranates and his skin is a map for the suffering in the days to come.

He extrudes all particles of the vast blue ocean layered in his skin and the salt he brushed off from it shall become a testimony of hard lives he lived.

She is collecting days in the crystal buckets to stir them with the detached salt from the Map-skin of young lad and waiting for the moment to kiss him in his forehead and transfer the entire salt of her ages for eternity and a day more.

Parthita Dutta
POLAND / INDIA

Parthita's debut book *The Boatman Beckons* was recently published by Notion Press, India. Her poetry has also published in several anthologies and magazines worldwide including: *Absolute Poetry Anthology* (UK), *Asia Sings Anthology* (Silk Road Literature), *Encyclopedia of a Thousand Poets: The Candles of Hope* (Tunisia), *Sindh Courier Web Portal for world Literature* (Pakistan), *Sungurlu Newspaper* (Turkey), *News Kashmir, Dainik Manob Kantha Patrika* (Bangladesh), *Litterateur International Magazine, Cultural Reverence International Magazine* and *Williwash Webzine.* She has also participated in several international virtual poetry meetings.
E: parthitadutta83@gmail.com
FB: @parthita.dutta
Instagram: @parthitadutta83

RESPECT

Any time if our paths are
destined to cross each other,
you would see me standing like
an Ellora sculpture to greet you:
hands folded, palm joined,
head bowed and pronouncing
the yogic word 'Namaskar.'
Don't ever think it is merely
for the sake of tradition;
it is beyond the surface notion
which I offer to you,
as the curtain-raiser
in that decorated platter.
A word, a simple word, greatly
reverberates within, I stand
in front of the mirrored soul;
a taint-less divine constituent
of your body, that I know, and see
 that reflected Supreme being
through your sheen, expressing
by piercing the layers of coloured coats,
manoeuvred mood, and opaque face,
and in submission, I bow my head
to show my regard and respect.

Amina Hrnčić
BOSNIA AND HERZEGOVINA

Amina has published two collections of poetry; *The Road to Agape* and *Octave*. Her book *The Road to Agape* was shortlisted among the first ten books for the Anka Topic Literary Award. Her poetry has been translated into German, and published in the Austrian journal *Lichtungen*, and in French for the Department of Slavic Studies at the Sorbonne University, Paris in 2021. The Gostivar Literary Festival translated her poetry and published it in Macedonian, and the festival Castello di Duino published her poetry in Italian. She is a three-time finalist of the Youth Poetry Festival, a finalist of Ratković's Poetry Evenings and Bulka Children's Poetry Festival. She was also shortlisted for the Slovo Gorčina award, and is the winner of several other literary awards in the region.
E: amina_hrncic@hotmail.com
FB: @amina.hrncic.5

Oči starije od ovog svijeta

Mi koji sumnjamo u legende,
Nikada nećemo razumjeti
Da nam je geometrija poklonjena,
I jednako sveta kao svijest,
Ni da je zaista najprije bila riječ,
Ista, odavdje do usamljenih plemena,
Koja još čuvaju žive priče na svojim jezicima,
I bježe u iskonski mir.

Figurina žene,
Iskustvo između prostora,
Riječi starije od ovog svijeta
Čijim znakovima
Nikada nećemo pronaći značenje,
I budne oči koje nas posmatraju,
U svakoj kući,
Oduvijek otvorene,
Uvijek uključene,

Tragovi u glini,

I sedam hiljada godina duboka
Potreba da sebe urežeš
U te velike oči
Koje se dive.

EYES OLDER THAN THIS WORLD

We who doubt in legends
Will never understand
That the geometry is a gift given to us
And as equally holy as consciousness,
Nor that there really was the word at the beginning,
The word that was the same
From here to the lonely tribes
Who still keep the living stories on their tongues
While they flee to the primordial peace.

Figurine of a woman.

The experience between spaces.
Words older than this world
With signs whose meaning
Will remain unknown
And those wondering eyes watching us
Looking at us in every home
Always open
Always included.

Traces in clay

And seven thousand years deep
Need to engrave yourself
In those big eyes
Who admire.

Hein Min Tun
MYANMAR

Hein Min Tun graduated from Mawlamyine University with a BA (Hons) degree in English Language & Literature in January, 2020, and is in the middle of doing his Master Degree. At the first outbreak of the global pandemic, when the universities were ordered to shut down nationwide, he embarked on the the life-long journey of writing; mostly poetry and short stories. Some of his works have been featured in popular international anthologies, and his poems *The Sound of Peace* and *The Day of Sunshine Will Come* were selected to go into *Timeless Inspirations.* His other works include *12 o' Clock (The Ambiguous Mind)* in the *Midnight Poetry Anthology*, *The Mirage* in the *Black Poetry Collection* and *Transience* in the *Garden of Poets*, all published by the Wingless Dreamer Publishing House. He is now working on his debut poetry book.
E: irisharold1211@gmail.com
FB: @Iris Harold

NOSTALGIA OF MY UP-COUNTRY LAND

When the sun sets over the upper countryside,
The desolate, dusty road of the village comes alive
With the jingles of an approaching bullock cart,
Wafted from afar through the crisp, cold early March breaths
Which flit across the verdant crop fields away
To the parched mouth of the village.

Peasants in cotton turbans come swaying on the tinkling cart
As it jerks along their village path,
Dimmed in the gloomy hue of the light-red sun;
Their wearied husbands lag behind who follow them on foot,
Shouldering soil-covered hoes and clasping open cane baskets.

Along their sluggish ride back home,
The women wipe off the tiny beads of sweats
Remaining on their foreheads and cheeks
With ragged, cotton handkerchiefs in sun-burnt hands
As they ruminate about their harsh day of sowing seeds
In the sesame plantation out in the scorching sun,
With subtle smiles which develop into giggles every now and then.

As the bull-cart passes by the marian and bombax trees
Which flank the village, teeming with vibrant blooms and ripened
fruits,
There loom up from a cluster of small huts in the distance
A line of beautiful village girls, neatly-braided and daintly dressed
In middle-sleeved checked outfits and colourful longyies;
Each carrying empty earthen water pots.
Their moon-bright faces adorned with Thanakha patches
Seem to be mocking at the magnificence of the western flame's
descent.
The young damsels shriek cheery greetings to their peers and fellow
villagers
As they strut past the indolent cart with elegant flair,
Leaving the aroma of their Thanakha clinging to the air
Which ripples through the blowing evening breeze
And strikes their sense of smell, relieving their day-long fatigue.

As the wooden cart clanks through
Bamboo, wooden and thatched houses
Squatting close to one another beyond the capacity of eyes,
The peasant-oil miller hail them with his unbounded smile

Who still busies himself guiding his ox round the circle
In the process of grinding peas for oil production.

Shabby children - some partially naked -
Have taken up much of the track of the cart
In their noisy, reckless frolic, intermingled with a few stray dogs
Which begin to bark at the sight of the bulls jingling into the village.
The bitter coldness of the March evening is brewing
As murky gloom drips from the dull, lead sky.
Overhead, boisterous pigeons and crows are fleeing
To evade the chilling sighs of the dusky air.
The peasants say goodbye and diverge homeward.
As evening progresses, darkness deepens.
The clangs from the copper gong rung in evening prayers
By the head monk from the monastery at the top of the village
Reverberate up into the heaven, rending the dark stillness.

As droopy night draws on, the pearly moon blooms,
Only revealing its partial aspect.
Fire lamps lighten the dark;
Beyond the open windows,
The young flames of candles and of oil lamps
Are drowsily stirring back and forth in the mischievous air.
When the quiet night sleeps over the village,
There come a flood of vague voices floating from the distant void
When tired women, accompanied by their offspring,
Happen to meet on the bamboo bench under the rain tree
With jaggery chunks and tea-leaf soup
To gossip in pleasure and muse on their past until the mid-hour
In the meagre glow of the frugal moon
With a dancing fire crackling and burning the night nearby.

Hannah Gates
CHINA / ENGLAND

Originally from Dorset, England, but is currently residing as an expat in the city of Suzhou, China, emerging poet Hannah was an avid reader from an early age, especially in the genres of romance, mystery and crime, and enjoys poetry, with Dylan Thomas and Lord Byron being amongst her favourites. She is a member of a local writers' group, and has contributed poems and a short story to an anthology on the theme of 'climate change.'
E: hannah1650@hotmail.com
W: www.landofsilkandhoney.net

REMEMBER YOUR P'S AND Q'S

Daffodils, triumphant in brazen yellow
Devotedly heralded spring
We were feeding the ducks
with pale, stale bread crusts in bags
We were rolling down the slopes, laughing
And there were signs on the pristine lawns
"Do not walk on the grass"

I remember the brown paper bags; crisp, crunching
Grapes from the green grocers, holding
We'd plant the stalk and in our naivety; hope for a tree

We made Easter gardens and pretty bonnets
I remember the musty odours of Sunday school carpets
Custard creams and orange squash for dunking
"Our Father, who art in heaven, hallowed be your name"
Behind cold wooden pews
On faded cushions, with the others we'd bow, kneeling
And a man with a red face like a permanent bee sting
Would jokily pinch off my nose.

They said I had a rose bud mouth
Peaches and cream complexion
"An English rose"

I remember the stone-grey ocean, in the dimness, lapping
Melancholy in the drizzle
Disappointed in the car on a cliff, sheltering
Across the window- pane; rain streaming
My hands hugging the warmth of a Cornish pastie

I remember the long, muddy walks
Stiles for climbing
Freezing streams for paddling
Feet were numb on the stepping- stones
"The fresh air's good for you" they'd say
"Don't forget to blow a kiss at the kissing gate in the grave- yard".
Country lanes laced with hedgerows winding
Abundant Blackberries for picking
Jam and pies for the making
In the long, light summer months

Piles of dead wood, ready for burning
Flames leaping, leaves falling
Flasks of tea, steam unfurling
Jacket potatoes, toffee apples, candy floss
Golden sparks in the dusk, dancing
Huge communal bonfires tempting
Us closer to warm our bodies in the chilly autumn air

Short, dark days ushered in winter
There were crumpets for tea on Sundays
And I remember how the butter, glistening
Sank slowly into the little holes, oozing
Like printing ink
I remember how they'd say:
"Elbows in, shoulders back!
Remember your P's & Q's!"

We borrowed a time-worn, wooden sledge
Down the Snow- blanket hills we were sliding
I remember the satsuma's citrussy scent in our stockings' ending
A rum- drenched figgy pudding with a tiny flame, quivering
Set alight; a brief, blue transparency

Eliza Segiet
POLAND

Eliza graduated with a Master's Degree in Philosophy, and has completed postgraduate studies in Cultural Knowledge, Philosophy, Arts and Literature at Jagiellonian University. Her poems *Questions* and *Sea of Mists* won the *Spillwords Press* title of International Publication of the Year 2017 and 2018, and *Sea of Mists* was chosen as one of the best amidst the hundred best poems of 2018 by *International Poetry Press Publication* Canada. In *The 2019 Poet's Yearbook,* as the author of *Sea of Mists*, she was awarded with the prestigious Elite Writer's Status Award, as one of the best poets of 2019, and her poem *Order* was selected as one of the 100 best poems of 2019. Eliza was nominated for the Pushcart Prize 2019, the iWoman Global Awards 2020, and the Laureate Naji Naaman Literary Prize, 2020. Her works can be found in anthologies and literary magazines worldwide.
E: eliza.anna@op.pl

PARALLEL TIME
To Mundara Koorangow
Translated by Ula de B.

With greatness
of multicoloured dots
not from alphabet Braille, Morse,
but from aboriginal tradition
the painted world
of ancient beliefs awes.
Ancestral past
united with today's day
tells a reality.

Parallel time
☐ magic between,
what was and what is found.

Dreamtime
doesn't permit forgetting.

No matter where you will start in your time.
What counts is where you'll make it
and what you'll hide in memory,
to be able to pass on to others.

Xavier Panadès I Blas
CATALONIA (SPAIN)

Xavier has been instrumental in the internationalisation of the culture of the Catalan Lands. His work is regularly published in international journals. and he is the author of the book of poetry *The Ear of Eternity* (Francis Boutle: 2019). Xavier is also an interpreter of poetry in Catalan, Castilian, and English, including the works of Blas de Otero, Federico García Lorca and Josep Vicenç Foix, and is regularly booked at festivals and online events such as Live Poets Society, Cerddi yn Cwrw/Pilsnerpoesi, and Like a Blot from the Blue. He is is currently working on translating and putting to music poems by Ramon Folch i Camarasa; the 20th anniversary re-edition of his first album *Per què no li dius? (Why don't you say?)*; and finalising the tracks of his upcoming album of poems.
E: xpan100@gmail.com
W: www. xpan.bandcamp.com
W: www.x-man.co.uk
FB: @SuperPanades
Instagram: @super_xavier
Twitter: @XPanades

Qui som?

Som l'arc de San Martí,
que mai el pots posseir,
que mai el pots tocar,
que mai el pots canviar.

Som el verd
dels boscs del Montseny,
de les alzineres balears,
de les hortes valencianes.

Som el groc
dels camps de gira-sols,
del sol que mai s'apaga,
de la flama de la lluita.

Som el negre
de la buidor de la mort,
de l'espai entre planetes,
de la mirada de la nit.

Som el roig
de la resiliència eterna
de la lluita perpètua,
de la rosa d'abril.

Som el blau
de l'escalfor de la mediterrània,
dels cels de la llibertat,
dels misteris de l'Estany de Banyoles.

Som aquell país
que de les pedres treure'n pans,
que fem castells en lloc de la guerra,
som els Països Catalans!

WHO ARE WE?

We are the rainbow,
you can never own it
you can never touch it,
you can never change it.

We are the green
of the forests of Montseny,
of the Balearic holm oak groves,
of the Valencian orchards.

We are the yellow
of the sunflower fields,
of the sun that never goes out,
of the flame of the struggle.

We are the black
of the emptiness of dead,
of space between planets,
of the gaze of the night.

We are the red
of eternal resilience
of perpetual struggle,
of the April rose.

We are the blue
of the heat of the Mediterranean,
of the heavens of freedom,
of the mysteries of the Lake of Banyoles.

We are that country
that we make bread out of the stones,
that we make castles instead of war,
we are the Catalan Lands!

Bruce Louis Dodson
SWEDEN

Bruce is an American expat living in Borlänge, where he writes novels, poetry, and creates collages. His most recent book, *Dearie-A Narrative Memoir*, was published January 2021. Other work he has appeared in includes: *Foreign & Far Away –Writers Abroad Anthology, Sleeping Cat Books-Trip of a Lifetime Anthology, Pirene's Fountain, Tic Toc Anthology-Kind of a Hurricane Press, Litro Magazine, Vine Leaves, Cordite Poetry Review, Buffalo Almanac, mgversion2>datura, So It Goes-Kurt Vonnegut Museum and Library, Smoky Blue Literature and Arts, Maintenant, Permafrost, Poetry Pacific, Canary, Vallum, Bangalore Review, Local Gems, Workers Write, NGY Review,* and *Whitefish Review*.
E: 2crows@earthlink.net
Blog: www.brucelouisdodson.wordpress.com

IMMIGRANT

I am almost the same as always
In this different place
Still unfamiliar
Customs, language, weather ... even humour
My world morphed in transit
Biggest change is
I will always be
Someone from somewhere else.
No common background with the locals
Memories of childhood and events
But something shared with
The growing numbers of the others
Like myself
Who moved from one place to another.

Dariusz Pacak
AUSTRIA / POLAND

Dariusz is a poet and essayist of Polish origin. He holds MFA Degree in Art (Poland, 1998), Professional Studies (Austria, 2000) and Hon. Doctor Degree of Literature (USA, 2011). He is a member of the World Academy of Arts and Culture (USA), Union of Polish Writers Abroad (Great Britain), Maison Naaman pour la Culture (Lebanon), World Nations Writers' Union, (Kazakhstan), and IG Autorinnen Autoren (Austria) His authored books include: *Birds of Emanations* (2001), *In Shattered Course of Things* (2003), *The House Of The Golden Fleece* (2004), *The Seasons* (2006), and has had work published in over 380 literary publications, magazines, anthologies and platforms worldwide.
E: pacakd@hotmail.com
FB: @dariusz.pacak.31

CONTEMPORARY DESOLATION
Translated from Polish by Ryszard J. Reisner

In the Figures Museum of Imagination
a decaying cross with Jesus
Allah's daily top of the pops
and absent steps of the Messiah
first temple silence of Shakyamuni

and the fading laugh of Godot
leave hope without life
a safe harbour for each of us
an empty place where meaning stops
in the Culture Museum of Civilisation

FILA VITAE
Translated from Polish by Ryszard J. Reisner

A stranger to endless gliding
freed from Europe decay delusion
I remove the West's blinker
under palm Taiwan roof and listen
the hand of Shakyamuni echoes
in marble Taroko ravines I blunder
only to find the way star-mapped
surrender to the Pacific roar
and light the light of Ēmítuó Fó
spanning a plank to out there
in Hui Chun's eyes of almond
Nirvana empty does not erupt
surrender shoulders spent
I clay jug of a heart
shatter the bell of Buddha
snared in newfound mirrors
a stranger from shore to shore.

IN SEARCH OF GODOT
Translated from Polish by Ryszard Reisner

She has dispensed one more affection
my vocation gave me 14 days notice
money has found a brand new billfold
my health decided to seek a better donor

all this bric-a-brac of mine
can be viewed
in The Museum of The Superfluous
where I decided to keep

Godly whims
be it April when it showers
and fortune good is fickle
be it gaudy March when it flowers

we blunder on the Way together
through swamps and marshes
where hours fork hearts lie empty
among unravelled whirlpools and storms

We blunder on
setting out to meet him on the Way

Rumyana Nikolova
BULGARIA

Rumyana has been a member of the Association of Plovdiv writers since 2006, and one of the founders of the intellectual poetic society Quantum and Friends. She has published two collections of poetry titled: *Reflections of Eternity* (2006) and *The Fifth Element* (2010), and her work has been published in a large number of international publications and platforms including: *Maritza, New Pulse, The Word Today, Birds at Night*, and *Antimov's Inn*, as well as in the *Among the sighs of butterflies'* literary collection, and the *Cultural Palette and Spirituality with no Boundaries* anthology.
E: rumy.nik@abv.bg

LIGHTNINGS – DAGGERS

A cloud – titan starts thundering with wings –
dripping wet, heavy with love …
The earth below is offering her fields
for him to stab with thunder – dagger after dagger …

And I – illuminated, reckless, like baptized,
grasp suddenly, enlightened by the thunder,
that days like those on finger-tips are counted
and pass away in our life elusive, in a dream …

WHENEVER YOU RING ME

Every fibre goes faint
with the dearest voice
and I melt in the ether
and my sense are lost.

In the blue pools of yours
under eyelashes silken
I am drowning, so save me
from unsavable dream.

You alone will come down
from the bank, on the moss –
only lips upon lips
will restore my breath lost.

Francis Otole
NIGERIA

Francis is a Nigerian born award-winning poet and academician. He is a graduate of the Benue State University, and a member of a number of literary groups including the Association of Nigerian Authors (ANA). His work has been featured locally, nationally and internationally in a large number of magazines, journals and anthologies.
E: otolefrancisnicholas@gmail.com
FB: @francis.otole

THERE WAS A COUNTRY

A country
that needs laundry:
A great nation
with impaired notion,
a deflated soul
beneath democracy's sole.
her conception
was deception.

Great leaders;
non- citizen readers.
crowned chiefs
and public thieves,
vibrant senates
and Luciferian innates,
gentle democrats
and manipulation technocrats,
stolen mandates
of genuine candidates.

dazed masses
of political passes,
confined helots
of power drunk harlots,
helpless destitute
of money mongering prostitutes,
opposition shooters
of public fund looters,
praise singers
of crooked democracy stingers.

Lynn White
WALES

Lynn is an English writer and poet living in north Wales. She was shortlisted in the Theatre Cloud 'War Poetry for Today' competition, and has been nominated for a Pushcart Prize and a Rhysling Award. Her poetry has appeared in many publications including: *Apogee, Firewords, Capsule Stories, Light Journal and So It Goes*. Her work is influenced by issues of social justice and events, places and people she has known or imagined. She is especially interested in exploring the boundaries of dream, fantasy and reality.
E: glanypwll3@googlemail.com
FB: @Lynn-White-Poetry-1603675983213077/
Blog: www.lynnwhitepoetry.blogspot.com

A GREY PLACE?

This is a grey place,
there's no denying.
Grey slate, grey granite,
grey houses built of both.
And it rains a lot, there's no denying.
Vertical, or horizontal, or swirling rain
falling greyly from heavy misty clouds.
But when caught by a sunbeam
it makes glistening slides
shimmering across the slate
and falls in bright white tails
or snakes like silver
where the mountains leak it.
And spills heavily over rocks,
it's foaming, frothing, yellow ruffed
cascades catching rainbows as they crash
then spitting them back out
in a fine spray of colours.
And now there's no grey
in the dark blue, black sky
filled with gold and silver twinkles.
No grey at all in this place now,
there's no denying.

First published by *Silver Birch Press* in *Where I Live Series,* 2015.

Stephen Kingsnorth
WALES

Stephen (Cambridge M.A., English & Religious Studies), born in London, retired to Wales from ministry in the Methodist Church with Parkinson's Disease, has had some 300 pieces published by on-line poetry sites, printed journals and anthologies, most recently *Academy of the Heart and Mind, The Parliament Literary Magazine, Runcible Spoon,* and *Poetry Potion*.
E: slkingsnorth@googlemail.com
W: www.poetrykingsnorth.wordpress.com

COMPASS

What is it causes me to verse,
conservative, and most, be frank,
both blank and bland, laid modern ways,
but rhyming rarely - best inside?
As faith in values built our home,
I was a rarity at school;
for I was steady as a boy,
wore jacket, tie at grammar school,
a swot, assuming that the norm,
capped eager for conformity,
where Bach outshone the Rolling Stones.
So given frame and leadership,
the discipline of uniform,
I camped and scouted, compass found,
a clear direction through the troop.
My mentor led me, apron strings,
for love of stagework brought its prize
with drama learned and Shakespeare played,
to Stratford, Dench and names like Dent
embossed, the spines of Everyman,
on shelves at home laid thick with tomes.
Whilst appetites were whet in form
with classics, poets, commonwealth -
Lepanto, Michael, Kubla Khan.
Morte d'Arthur, written laureate,
old order giving place to new
came Hopkins, Gerard Manley, priest,
a metric breathing, rhythms sprung,
bright coloured words, terms standing proud,
pied beauty, Hughes and Spender's hues.
Through love of language, Cambridge called,
a privilege intense and broad;
and there vocation intervened
with grappling theological,
as station in the pulpit came,
with public speaking, words proclaimed
as art in oratory performed.
And now, sat down from preaching rôle,
enforced by Parkinson's decree,
that compass set, magnetic key,
free days to write and versify.

STANDARD

For Queen and country, loyalty,
but what's the call, for those who die?
The flag, united ground and field,
from hoist to fly end, royal blue,
by history, three saints imposed.
Red, white and blue, unique to none,
to build or cut the ties that bind,
yet sign that waves from pride to fear -
a standard, shamed in empire's tide?
I walk the line, a middle road,
the corrupt strain less bad than done,
and thankful not, some others' sum -
freedom to stand up for the count
in ballot box and protest songs,
though wider gap from rich to poor,
complacency the wolf at door.
A faith, root welfare, in the state,
a commonwealth of global bounds,
and literature for every taste,
in arts and science, partnerships.
Folds, nestling hills, a village spire,
a climate yet of moderate;
but can we navigate our course
down country lanes to mindful ways?

URBAN SWERVE

My teenage, borne in urban scape
by serendipity, in stealth,
effected move to moorland heath.
Mount orange box, guide skipping rope,
bold pavement swerves, clipped city kerbs,
week's shopping bags, strewn apples, leeks -
old go-cart gave way, hiking boots,
that axle burn turned abseil hold.

I longed for yells, clear crowds from path,
big points for scare, here mine alone -
heard belay calls, rock climbing face,
slow rise to rush adrenalin.
Nail granite bite, one toe tip grip,
supplanted by wind rush, tor top,
curbed charm of snaking coil below,
saw route, sail reservoir, canoe.

Words tack and boom, with crampon spikes,
set rhyming slang took on fresh voice,
with burr and rolling singing slurs,
an adolescent culture twist.
Across the tracks, my circuit mates,
paroled their streets, fixed terms fulfilled;
but I, transferred to peat moss, grouse,
had no complaints, new venture paths.

Sanjana Karthik
CANADA / INDIA

Sanjana is an entrepreneur, leader of organizations, writer and TV show host. She dedicates her spare time to volunteering, where she has accumulated over 1000 hours. She tutors, and provides leadership services to Volunteer Club, Study Circle, and Medhopeful at her school. She has created an organization called Your Words Matter To Us, co-founding an upcoming mental health app called myEsprit, and creates mental health campaigns through the BC Youth Council. Above all, her passion lies in writing poetry, where she writes for *Reclamation Magazine, BC Youth Council*, and *GenZ Writes* and various other places. Her work has been read by the Mayor of Whiterock, and shared on various magazines and radio shows. She also hosts her own show on *CloseLook* called the *Reality Is*, and is grateful to be able to combine her passion for advocacy, mental health, public speaking and writing.

E: skarthik.study@gmail.com

AN INDIAN GIRL

I used to feel
Uncomfortable
In my own skin

My dark brown hue
And even my kin

I longed to be white
A product of systematic racism
I longed to feel accepted
But instead was locked in a prison

Of my mind

Of my culture
Feeling
Less than divine

Worrying about tanning
Worrying about police brutality
Worrying about feeling like an outcast
I lost my sanity

Not being represented in books
Eyes gaze through
When we were younger

Feeling like an exception
As opposed to society's member

TO MY INDIAN PARENTS

You take care of us
Not thinking twice
Showering us
With unconditional love
At no price

You love with all your heart
And so does the child
Until days turn to years
And so do your fears

The children become distant
And reserved
They discover love
In wrong places
Trying to quench avoid

And replace you ...

You poured your soul,
Your blood,
And time

And they just depart

Distance filling the gaps
As they try to create a new life

To my parents-
If I ever made you feel this way,
Or made you question
Whether I love you

Please know
You are my most treasured people
And with each new day
Is a vow to never hurt you

MY LOVING INDIAN FAMILY

You are an alluring warmth,
A beautiful glow,
Radiant and promising,
Hovering over us with your gold

Cascading as an angle
From our window to the floor
Gleaming on the family table
Heartbeats-
Never ignored

An affirmation,
A comfort,
Through arguments
That persist

That even when rains come over
You are opened like a door

Always there,
Holding the day,
Shielding me
From our thunderstorm

You are my family;
A warm little glow
And the merest of conversations
We share

Make me feel whole-

Cheryl-lya Broadfoot
ENGLAND

Cheryl-lya is an avid Soul Adventurer. Created and raised in Johannesburg, South Africa, she is now based in London. Her first adventures began in the classroom, daydreaming instead of learning, writing and poetry were always secret loves … Chocolate and tea-lover, usually found helping women launch successful and sustainable businesses, she has been known to caress the realms of the typed-word occasionally (as a novice). She loves to follow her own soul's compass, and in doing so has found herself entertaining people with her short-stories and poems. She is self-published, twice, in self-help and a number of times in various anthologies. She is researching her third self-help book. On her journey she has met a host of writing-angels (human and celestial) all busy helping her grow her global snowball of happiness through as many means as possible, despite a number of health concerns. She carries on regardless, and enjoys it!
E: souls_compass@yahoo.com
W: www.wellbeingshowcase.com
W: www.soulscompass.net

WHO AM I?

In a rainbow nation I was born innocent, lover of unicorns,
magical beasts of myth and a mystery that take the sting out of our
history.
Then I grew old enough to vote, together a new history we wrote.
As the years moved on, I grew to find the place where I belong,
no longer scared to speak my mind
nor attack actions deemed unkind.
Now my adult self has found, a neutral ground
where freedom sounds.
Still not clear of who I really am
or if I'll ever lose the role of 'meek lamb'.
Somehow I'll learn to speak my truth,
and to soothe my words with peace.
Not sure where I'm going or where I'll land,
the only certainty being life is unplanned.
Happier knowing I'm a global mix, and despite the politics,
I'll always be a third world child,
full of mystery, magic and bit self-styled:
born of the Rainbow Nation, a living global co-creation.

HOME

Trying to write a poem about my home, sitting in the cold, all alone.
Confused, bemused and trying to find my way around life … feeling blind.
Do I write about my land of birth, of golden sunny days, rooibos and resources of worth?
Or do I write about the land which matured me, helped me into adulthood and set me free?
Two lands nine-thousand miles apart, each distinctive, both held firmly in my heart.
In a way, both birthed me, nursed me, formed me.
With a foot in each hemisphere, suddenly I see that home is where the heart is, a state of mind:
living life, doing good, being kind, making contrasts blend as one.
The dissonances done – a new life has begun.
And now I finally feel 'home', no longer feeling alone.
Together we are family where many worlds are lived as one, we all belong.

ANYONE THERE?

Born white in a middle class house to working class parents who made it,
barely ... not really.
In a land forgotten, boycotted and rotten,
until '94 that magical year when all became free and equal and
rights were fair and together we stood tall and proud.
Until contracts were won through bribery and corruption.
Nepotism ran rife, soon nothing, nil, zero became the worth of a life.
People left hungry and scared and promises still
as empty and hollow as the echoes of time.
The world stopped singing for us and moved to another cause,
we stood still listening ... our lives on pause, waiting for the applause,
the acceptance from world leaders and those in power around the globe.
Instead we were laughed at, a joke,
our currency status soon became junk – who woulda thunk?
And now the beauty, the majesty is just another travesty as
fraud by Maude because she's Gucci-devoid is the norm.
And black and white and Indian and mixed are left behind
to work and work and one day to jerk
awake and see they have enough money to flee
and those left behind who can't see the signs
yet stay and fight
hoping to not be the last one out, to turn out the light
as they bid South Africa good night.

Jake Aller
SOUTH KOREA

John (Jake) Cosmos Aller grew up in Berkeley, California, and Washington and is a retired U.S. Foreign Service Officer currently living in South Korea. He served in ten countries over a 27-year career with the Department of State. He graduated from the University of Washington with an MPA degree and a MA in Korean studies, and did his undergraduate work at the University of the Pacific in Political Science and Psychology. Before his diplomatic career, John taught ESL, Government, and Asian studies in Korea with the University of Maryland and Kyunghee University. He also served in the Peace Corps in Korea.

E: authorjakecosmosaller@gmail.com
W: www.theworldaccordingtocosmos.com
Twitter: @jakecaller

MY MOTHER'S HISTORY

One day many a year ago
My mother spoke to me
About her family's tangled history,

She spoke to me
Of lies, half-truths, and myths
Some of which may have been true
And throughout the evening
Her history came alive.

She was born in the hills
of North Little Rock
The 10th of 11 children
Of an ancient dying race.

The Cherokees
who had run away
Refusniks
Refugees who fled in the hills.

Part of the lost tribe of the Cherokee nation
Part Cherokee, Choctaw, Creek, Seminole
and African Americans
Who fled to the mountains
To avoid the trail of tears.

Rather than join the rest
In the promised land
Of Oklahoma.

They did not exist
I did not exist.

The BIA told us
No Indian scholarship
For you

Since you can't prove
You are in fact
Of Native American ancestry,

I asked my mother

What does this mean?
She said

No BIA money for you,
My non-Indian son.

Her family and Bill Clinton family
Were related
Bill Clinton and I are distant cousins

When I met him
I related my family history
He concluded that we were indeed cousins
Said I could call him Cousin Bill
And he would call me Cousin Jake

And he too was part Cherokee
Irish, Scotch, French
And African American
Part of the lost tribe
Of the Cherokee nation

I told my mom
This story
She said
It was true

She was a distant cousin
Of Bill Clinton
Still did not like
The lying SOB

Her people disappeared
From history's eyes
And DNA data banks

My history was over
As was hers
And so,
I learned at last
The painful truth

That due to the geocidal crimes
of politicians so long ago
My mother's people

Lost their land, their culture,
and their hope
And became
downtrodden forgotten people

Hillbillies they were called
Living in the hills and mountain dales
Clinging to the dim fading memories
Of their once glorious past
As proud Cherokees

Now no one knew their name
The old ways were forgotten
And the new world never forgave them

And they never forgave the new world
As they lived on
In the margins of society
Forgotten people

And I vowed that as long as I lived
Their history would not die
As I knew the truth

And I would become a proud
Cherokee
And make my mother proud of me
And my accomplishments

When I am down and out
I recall her stories and her warnings
And realize it is up to me

To live my life
To let the Cherokee in me
Live his life

And in so doing
My mother's history does not die
It lives on in me
Until the day I die

Long live the Cherokee nation
Long live my mother

Stefan Markovski
NORTH MACEDONIA

Stefan is a contemporary North Macedonian writer, poet, screenwriter, and philosopher, and the author of novels, short story collections, poetry, and theoretical books. He has an MA in Screenwriting at the Faculty of Dramatic Arts (FDU), and is a member of Macedonian Writers' Association, the Macedonian centre of the International Theatre Institute, the European poetry platform Versopolis, and other international associations. He's the chief editor at *Sovremenost* - the oldest Macedonian literary magazine – as well as the poetry collections of the project *Metric Caravan*, published by the municipal library in Gevgelija. Stefan has authored over a dozen scientific papers in international scientific journals on literary science, stylistics and philosophy, and his works have been translated into a number of languages. The English translations of his novels *The Bumblebee Anatomy* and *Letters of Heresy*, his collection of short stories titled: *Faustus Runs the Plebeian Circle*, and the poetry collection *Promised Land*, have all achieved notable success.
E: markovskistefan@gmail.com
FB: @stefan.markovski.165

OUR ASHES

Our ashes are dust on the bodies of the
intact gods,
a shadow that builds
all the world's heavens,
a flag waiting to be lifted
by the wind in between
that only sometimes moans out loud.

Our ashes hide the sunwords
in an Easter basket braided with red thoughts,
our ashes precede the gray shine
of foreign universes once purified
by moments of water and grains of fire
our ashes are being crumbled in chrome plates
from the dining rooms of the homes of
children who are not yet born,
light as the earth protecting us.

PROMISED LAND
To the departed

Like compasses for unreachable paradises
ancient dreams shall show towards
the undug light lands of the inmost
the great winds that'll ward off
seven holy days will not pass without a shadow
in the room we will not seek the silence
that afflicts and heals
in the hospitals where voices are blowing
merry science won't kill anymore
the gods in our heads.
Silk universes of childhood shall flutter
with the sunset
which is to be hugged from the shadows of the bodies
crucified under the time that rains futures.

Still undawned
blue voids shall burn
from the shrines out of control
young age
will slowly get replaced by
the colours of wide-awakeness
that's running in
front of a locomotive dragging the years
which break you free
from freedom that illuminates lights
We are adult and now
empty is the cradle of the lost winds
there are no children of the truth
nor perfect illusions
the letter "o" becomes air
exhaled from the chest of a fallen revolutionary
matured in-between fields wed with blood,
confined with night.

And yet, an attempt and a hope is our
golden trek for eternity
and everything that listens
to the ancestral torment
in an embrace with these lands
everything from the reflection of this hour
truth again shall it be.

Tis for us not to know
what is
the strength of the cursed
the idyll of the departed;
to see it as a southern flower in June
in the middle field of the fallen homeland
the white vigour of the exiled
in promised lands of the lost notes
and voices with shadows of envy.

It is for us to condemn it
from the first revelation
the tremor of the weak
ostensibly strange is only the fear resembling guilt
metaphysics and thought
build rifts
in meat ramparts
promised land
a promised land finds the sight buried in itself
a sight, echo of a voice saying the promised land
is hidden by the stride of the living,
the fatigue of the deers
and the embrace of every half-sun with the gorges
which confine clarity of the early days.

Promised Land
whose dawn is the one
when the clouds
grow up in the golden plows of the boundlessness
and rains call for life in the desolation
          - Logs in the time of the departed.

Oh my promised Land ...

Ndaba Sibanda
ETHIOPIA / ZIMBABWE

Originally from Bulawayo, Zimbabwe, but now living in Addis Ababa, Ethiopia, Ndaba is the author of *Notes, Themes, Things And Other Things, The Gushungo Way, Sleeping Rivers, Love O'clock, The Dead Must Be Sobbing, Football of Fools, Cutting-edge Cache, Of the Saliva and the Tongue, When Inspiration Sings In Silence, The Way Forward, Sometimes Seasons Come With Unseasonal Harvests, As If They Minded: The Loudness Of Whispers, This Cannot Be Happening: Speaking Truth To Power, The Dangers Of Child Marriages:Billions Of Dollars Lost In Earnings And Human Capital, The Ndaba Jamela and Collections* and *Poetry Pharmacy*. Ndaba's work has received Pushcart Prize and Best of the Net nominations. Some of his work has been translated into Serbian.
E: loveoclockn@gmail.com

A WOMAN AT WORK

Her brain is on the grain that is being prepared
and processed. There is no maze in a common
sight and sound as the maize grain is threshed
and pounded by crude mortar and pestle.

She is grinding corn in a mortar. A mother of 5,
in a village where the mill is far, she has no
choice but to manually process all her grain.
It is a backbreaking, laborious chore.

She learnt the traditional principles of hulling
and milling when she was a little girl since
her parents couldn't afford paying for
commercial grain-milling services.

She knows the importance of food production,
the goal of milling: enhancing the digestibility
of the grain for human consumption,
to produce a grainy, palatable meal.

Her pestle weighs 4 kg and the pounding task
is sweat, toil, time and energy. It is an effort.
Mortar and pestle are a pair moulded
from a tree stump and branch.

Ioannis Adnan Karajoli

GREECE / SYRIA

Ioannis is a Greek poet based in Thessaloniki. Born and spending his early childhood in Afrin, a city north of Aleppo, Syria, his family is of Kurdish origin. His mother was an artist, and his father a writer and lawyer, who fought for the rights of the Syrian people. Ioannis studied at the Bucharest Dentistry School in Romania, and specialised as an Orthodontist. After graduating, he moved to Greece after being invited there by his fellow Greek students. His first poetic collection was published in 2011 under the title *Shades of an Era*. His second poetic collection titled *Hellenic speech, Light of the World* was published in 2018. He then went onto publish *The Daughter of the North* followed by *The Moon of the Orient*. His latest poetic collection is titled *Love And Tenderness*. He received an Honorary Distinction at the 4th International Poetic Contest for his collection *Hellenic speech, Light of the World* (Thessaloniki, May, 2014), He is a member of the Litterateurs Association of Northern Greece, and of the cultural institution: Amphictyonic League of Hellenism. He has lectured at; the 3rd International Amphictyonic Congress on The History of Hellenic-Syrian Culture, that took place at the French Institute of Thessaloniki (May, 2014); on Language and Communication at the festival Celebration of Multilingualism (Thessaloniki, May, 2014); and, with his poem titled *Smyrna*, at the 1st Pan-Hellenic Contest.
E: karazolijohn@gmail.com

MY BELOVED HOMELAND

I love you
even from a distance. I look at you
with the falcon's vision that looks backwards.
I live with the scents of your beautiful past I borrow the spring
that looks like your own so as to feel
at home
even for a little while. Half of me
is a bird
that flies into your sky at night,
to protect you
from any mysterious enemy of yours. My other half
is a skeleton
that lives in Europe.
He borrows your traditional clothes
to use as a blanket and as a protection against the cold winter and
the foreign land. In the evenings I walk by the seashore
gazing at scenes from Latakia, Tartus and Banias.
The sea breeze brings me that scent of the sea
and the sweet-smelling jasmine of our evenings.
I can still hear
the neighbours' and the old men's chats.
I can still hear the noise of the worry beads
that the old man deftly plays between his fingers under the street
post
and suddenly I long to run towards my home
to my parents'
arms,
Syria – Greece.

Mark Andrew Heathcote
ENGLAND

Mark is from Manchester. His poetry has been published in many journals, magazines and anthologies worldwide, and is the author of *In Perpetuity* and *Back on Earth,* two books of poems published by a CTU publishing group - Creative Talents Unleashed. Mark is an adult learning difficulties support worker, who began writing poetry at an early age at school.
E: mrkheathcote@yahoo.co.uk

WHO AM I?

Who am I, am I, a savant
am I, a guardian of knowledge or a fool?
Am I an uninhabited sapphire moon?
Or a sentinel of fire & carnal desire:

Who am I, am I, a philosopher
a great man of thoughts, a scholar
or a boxing ring ringer.

Who am I, am I, a poet sage
if I am, do I care about my age?
It's true; I don't suffer jealousy
And I'm healing all my rage
the captivity of a bear locked in a cage.

Who am I, am I, a guru
could all this misery be?
Another kind of voodoo-
or is it a Juju gift?
A kind of magician's magic
who am I really, answer you're just a son of man?

Tetiana Grytsan-Czonka
UKRAINE

Tetiana is the author of 11 collections of poetry, and the novel-essay *Living Doors, or I - the blind Apple of the ages. I am a Woman.* Member of the All-Ukrainian public organization LO Kobzar, the National Union of Writers of Ukraine, and International Academy LIK, she is also the co-author of 57 Ukrainian and international anthologies and almanacs including: *Article, Tel Aviv, Soul* (Japanese poetry collection), *Brzegi Ognia i Wody* (Polish almanac), literary and art magazine *TextOver,* international collection of poetry about peace *Lily Marlene*, Greek collection *Hellas*, Chinese collection *Poetry of the World*, textbook for Ukrainian students *Modern literature of the native land*, and author of the Azerbaijani-Ukrainian poetry collection *Golden apple*, and others. She has also won a number of awards and competitions, in particular: Laureate of the Panteleimon Kulish International Literary and Artistic Prize (2020) - for the book of prose *Living Doors, or I am a ripe apple of the ages, I am a Woman,* Laureate of the international competition *Pushkin and Gogol in Italy*, Laureate of the International Prize Franz Kafka, Laureate of the International Golden Feather Award in Azerbaijan, and others.
E: tet-a-tetana@ukr.net

Життя

Як святість, що опікує сльозами,
До схилу, до небес, до мами...
До жовтої із небом глини, Людино,
Чого тобі іще потрібно?
Ти в межи плідні, ти за рідних
Повзеш лозою, носиш спомин,
Ти знаєш до, ти відаєш про вчора,
А не приймаєш нині...
Надто рівна дорога вийшла перед тебе.
Чого тоді, чого ще треба?
Людина не знає відради,
До білого світу
Людина привнесла принади,
Людина вийшла з пекла в рай,
Людина написала вкрай
Важливу строчку...
Людина одягла сорочку,
Людина вибілила гривні...
 Тепер уже лиш час і ливні
Напишуть про її життя.

LIFE

As a saint who cares for tears,
To the slope, to heaven, to moum ...
To the yellow clay with the sky, Man,
What else do you need?
You are fruitful, you are for relatives,
You crawl through the vine, you carry the memory,
You know before, you know about yesterday,
And you do not accept today ...
The road is too flat in front of you.
What then, what else is needed?
Man does not know the joy,
To the white world
The man brought charms,
Man came out of hell into heaven,
The man wrote extremely
Important line ...
The man put on a shirt,
Man bleached hryvnias ...
Now it's time for showers
They will write about her life.

Kakoli Ghosh
INDIA

Kakoli Ghosh (a.k.a. Moon Drops) is a post-graduate in English literature. She is a multilingual writer: many of her poems in vernacular Bengali language have been published online and in local magazines. She has self-published a poetry book titled *Unfinished from Durban, South Africa,* and one of her poems, *Grains of Salt*, was published in a South African anthology *Poems for Haiti*. Her work has been published in various anthologies including: *Paradise on Earth: Vols. I & II, Ferring Love,* and *Glomag.*
E: kakolimajumdarghosh@gmail.com
FB: @moon.drops.773
Instagram: @moondrops_2020

SCRIPTURES

The station road house
among the sudden cluster of green,
beyond the carefree mud lane
by the promising stream,
gave the fecund horizon a theme.

The twilights, calm as a new bride,
hesitant at the night's door
stood with downcast eyes;
a purple dusky scent did adore
the far stretching paddy fields ashore.

Conch shell was blown to greet God.
Scriptures of time on granny's face
came alive in the oil lamp flicker,
she held it at the 'tulsi' altar,
an auspicious herb of heaven's grace.

Her indistinct holy chants in whisper
which nobody but Gods can decipher
were as innocent as a child's prattle,
uttered lovingly whatever
would be understood by its mother.

Framed Gods with unframed bliss,
ranging from images to clay idols
in a small wooden cabinet did stay.
Regular sandalwood paste on them
flaked granny's fingerprints everyday.

Sugar candies offered on tiny plates
nourished heaven in her God's cage.
Greedy cockroaches, plump lizards
enlivened the incense smoke haze,
wise ants fulfilled their sweet targets.

Neil Leadbeater
SCOTLAND

Neil is an author, essayist, poet and critic. His short stories, articles and poems have been published widely in anthologies and journals both at home and abroad. His publications include *Librettos for the Black Madonna, The Worcester Fragments, The Loveliest Vein of Our Lives, Sleeve Notes, Finding the River Horse, Punching Cork Stoppers, River Hoard, The Engine-room of Europe* and *Penn Fields*. He is a regular reviewer for a number of other journals including *Write Out Loud* (UK), *The Halo Halo Review* (USA), *Quill & Parchment* (USA), and *Contemporary Literary Review India* (India).
E: neil.leadbeater1@virginmedia.com

LEAVING NEW STREET

Beyond the tunnels there were factories and cranes, a compendium
of car parks, junk yards, tips; bulldozers shifting history.
Tower blocks bestrode the landscape. The Monday wash,
draped over railings, dried in the midday heat.

Along the way, a series of signs in quick succession
told us where we were at: *Smethwick Rolfe Street - Smethwick
Rolfe Street - Smethwick Rolfe Street -*

The summer haze, airless and venal,
congealed with the log-jam of trade:
foundries, lighting and switchgear; dossils, plugs and valves;
they put back in place all those things
that I thought I had nearly lost:
the smell of malt from a Midlands brewery,
the red marl of the back-to-backs; a school bell in a comprehensive
ringing me back to Maths.

I lived here once, much as I lived in other towns
but none has brought me back so much as this -
nosing the scent of something gone,
the past we always miss.

RENTON ROAD ALLOTMENTS

Renton Road Allotments were on the other side of town
somewhere you'd never been to
but it conjured up the conviviality
of mixing with people from different cultures
who shared a passion for plants -
the Indian amid the still expanse of Exbury hybrid azaleas;
Jamaicans with their summer squashes
huggermugger with massed astilbes
ranged between the beans
and a small child
bad-mouthing belladonna
because his father had told him
it was the only fruit in the town grounds
of which he could not eat.

A MIDLANDS ALPHABETUM

Abercrombie Street.
Builders' merchants
Clocking-on.
Daybreak cracks them open; it sandbags them into
Elemental labour while next door's
Foundry fires a slab of
Galvanized iron into a
Hot-rolled metal bar. The sum of their lives
Inches off the production line. It makes them
Jump the queue at the works canteen for a
Kit-Kat snack on the hoof. Across the street a
Lone operative smokes away her well-earned break while a
Manufacturer of scrap compaction
Number-crunches the working day into a state of abject
Oblivion. Wesley's
Pressworks padlocked-off.
Quiet nights
Rolling down like Venetian blinds on the
Storm water attenuation tanks; keys
Turning in back doors. Lighting-
Up time. The night shift cascading into focus.
Voices off. A boxful of
Widgets, plugs and spigots, the
Xerox copier shuttling sheets back and forth like
Ying and yang or the strung string of the Yo-yo, the spark of
Zinc in the zero-hour; dark glass after midnight.

Masudul Hoq
BANGLADESH

Masudul has a PhD in Aesthetics under Professor Hayat Mamud, Jahangirnagar University, Dhaka. He is a contemporary Bengali poet, short-story writer, translator and researcher. His previous published work includes short stories *Tamakbari* (1999), *The poems of Dhonimoy Palok* (2000), *Dhadhashil Chaya*, which translated version is *Shadow of Illusion* (2005) and *Jonmandher Swapna* which translated version is *Blind Man's Dream* (2010), translated by Kelly J. Copeland. Masudul also translated T.S. Eliot's poem *Four Quartets* (2012) and Allen Ginsburg's poem *Howl* (2018) from English to Bengali. In the late 1990s, for three years he worked under a research fellowship at The Bangla Academy. Bangla Academy has published his two research books. His poems have been published in Chinese, Romanian, Mandarin, Azarbaijani, Italian, Russian, Turkish, Nepali and Spanish. At present he is a Professor of Philosophy in a government college.
E: masudul.hoq@gmail.com

LAMP OF ALADDIN

A lamp shining

There is no one else in the Arabian night
Only me and the lamp

At best I'm a moth
The lamp as a sun

In the lure of a little more light
Rubbing on the lamp
The monster comes out

Since then I have been Aladdin;
The story of Aladdin is going on
The monster is just mine!

Eduard Schmidt-Zorner
REPUBLIC OF IRELAND / GERMANY

Eduard is a translator and writer of poetry, haibun, haiku, and short stories. He also writes under his pen-name Eadbhard McGowan. He writes in four languages: English, French, Spanish, and German, and holds workshops on Japanese and Chinese style poetry and prose and experimental poetry. Member of four writer groups, he has been published in over 160 anthologies, literary journals, and broadsheets in USA, UK, Ireland, Australia, Canada, Japan, Sweden, Spain, Italy, France, Bangladesh, India, Mauritius, Nepal, Pakistan, and Nigeria. Some of his poems, and haibun have been also published in French (own translation), Romanian, and Russian. Originally from Germany, he has lived in Ireland for more than 25 years, and is a proud Irish citizen.

E: EadbhardMcGowan@gmx.com
FB: @Eadbhard McGowan

HERITAGE AND ORIGIN

When the ambient air
influences genes, then
Wrzészcz is in my blood:
forests, heather fields,
the aroma of Kashubian cod
and flounders with potatoes
or the scent of fish soup
with bread, butter, sour cream.
A dream strongly anchored
and etched
into my subconscious -
burning longing for *Gdańsk*
and the Baltic coast -
this desire is like a tiny fly
enclosed
in a drop of amber.

YELLOWED MEMORIES

Snow-covered fields lie wide
on which playful crows are dancing.
Deep stretches the countryside
up to the frozen hem of the horizon
uniting with the Baltic Sea.
Drains and ditches, silver lanes,
willow trees, wizen.
A buzzard hovers over the plains.

A picture book takes childhood by the hand;
memories settle as dust on what remains.
Sun penetrates through roof beams
into an imaginary faded wonderland.
There it is, my island under dreams:
Endless *taiga*, abundant clouded lake land.

Would like to hide, seek shelter, in fields of rye,
or between those thumbed pages of a fairy tale,
star money coins like rosary beads recounting,
pass through my fingers, dreamily,
to pay for moonlight over the *Curonian Spit*
and the *Vistula* river.

The memory suitcase gets heavier,
heart grows old
a thousand nights since passed,
counted by falling calendar sheets,
the hair grows white, open fields are cold,
a broken cross warns at the waterside.

Only thoughts remain on yellowed photos:
A forlorn couple with me
in front of green pine forests.
A lonely house near marshy meadows.
The step beyond the horizon not far away.

CALLING YOUR NAME

I never knew my grandfather,
never made his acquaintance
or felt his affection, his closeness.
I talk often to the dead,
try to share moments, explain my fears,
or to ask for their opinion.

I speak to them to make a connection.
Will they answer me from a distance?
Do they know my apprehension?
Hard to hear them in the noise
of this side's distracting diversions.

I imagine an old man with white hair
holding my hand, smiling,
as we walk through streets,
lined with chestnut trees,
and pass through wheat fields;
he is talking to me or remains silent.

Silence is often an answer
to questions whose response
would be too elusive.
In this dream we have a dialogue:
he explains things to me
and I ask hundreds of questions
to discover an unknown domain.

We have now a conversation
between rows of graves,
where startled deer watch the living
who search for traces of the dead,
stand motionless on the clearing
of this peaceful location, so soothing,
that even the hind and the fawn
are surprised to hear steps
on the carpetlike lawn.

I would have liked to listen to him,
to his experience and vast knowledge.
He suffered two wars,
survived the first, lost a son and a daughter.

He did not see the end of the second,
nor Hitler's death which he yearned for.
Nothing remained of him:
He not only lost his life.
He lost everything.

Only a handful of ashes is left
in a plot, one meter by one meter,
with a simple headstone.

I have a yellowed photo,
mounted on brown cardboard.
At the bottom, it says:
Atelier Raspe
Imperial court photographer 1894
an illegible address on the reverse side,
handwritten in Gothic script.
His permanent address now is:
Central Cemetery,
field twelve, row eight, grave thirty.

UNCOMPLETED FORM OF A MIGRANT

The snail is carrying its house on the back,
moving from A to B in slow motion,
a straight line, no diversion.
My route, though, was never straight.

Inquisitiveness of official questionnaires
asking for details.
I offered locations unfit for official forms.
Where born, parents, education, town,
yes or no?

Yes, born in an unprecedented winter,
where the freezing were starving,
and the starving were freezing
in borrowed beds.

Packed suitcases, no address.
Train stations.
Russian officers looked into my pram.
I laughed at them. "Lucky child", they said.
Ice flowers on the window,
a dead cat in a ruined house.
Where were you born?
Not enough space in the form.
Pure coincidence the answer ... too long a word.

Locations hesitantly spelling.
Gdańsk, Wiślinka, Wrzeszcz.
Proof of evidence:
Please tick the appropriate box(es)!
A snail has a house...we found a shelter
in a rat-infested cellar.

Nationality.. asks the form.
(a snail has no nationality,
only leaves a shiny trace).
As a yet unborn traveller, I crossed the lands:
Pomerania, Saxony, Kashubia, ...
under Russian hands.

Parents had to wait four years for passports.
Nationality then:

wanderer between destroyed lands.
Eternal transit, a life-long journey,
restlessly roaming
with uncompleted forms in hand.

Penitential wanderings and odysseys,
as the fate of Saint Brendan demonstrated
to end where <u>he</u> started: in Ireland.

Cead Mile Failte a successful marketing trick
to lure people, who come and go and do not stay.
"I hope they do not stay"
I heard so often, "they take our jobs away."

Got citizenship after five years of good behaviour
Integrated, assimilated,
pretended once to be Irish, on an art poster
me "the Irish artist"
the word "Irish" was deleted with a black marker
the next day
And I once dared to say:
I am a Kerryman now.
The reaction: Imposter, I was told,
Imposter, the new nationality.

Ivana Radojičić
SERBIA

Ivana is a writer, poet, iconographer, translator, public health specialist and multimedia artist. Her work has been published in a number of online and print magazines including *011info*. She has also published a novel titled: *Sifra Ceremonyal* and is finishing a second.
E: gorodecki.a@gmail.com
FB: @ivana.b.radojicic
Instagram: @ivana_radojicic_art

GRAVEYARDS

Sometimes,
I visit my dead.
Stand over the stone that covers the ones before me.
The two of them are in a vase now.
He came to Belgrade as a child.
By train.
To a concentration camp.
She burned her only shoes why trying to dry them in a stove.

I turn my face catching the warmth of the sun.
Like a flower,
Rooted in the vase with ashes.
The dust that holds my burned genes,
My burned love,
My burned hugs.
My live memories.

I never visit my great grandfather.
He is dead too.
But is not in a vase.
He is buried in the meadow,
There,
Up on that hill.
He was murdered and put in the ground there.
His wife went mad,
And my love from the vase
Lost her father.

My grandmother has the best view.
She has her commodity in her tomb
On the hill,
Overlooking the Boka Kotorska bay.
Where her family once had big sailing ships,
It is such a lively place.
Such a pity that she is dead.

But, I am still walking these grounds.
With those from the ground sitting in my ribcage.
Sometimes,
I give them my eyes,
So we can watch the wonders of the world together.

THE SON

My grandparents called me their son,
just like their parents called them.
But I am a girl.

I loved my grandfather's gentle voice
whispering in my ear
"You are so beautiful, my son"

Now it is nearly a sin to call your daughter a son,
Still,
I am a girl, who loved being called a son.

John Tunaley
ENGLAND

John was born in Manchester in 1945. Father: foundry hand, mother; crane-driver is what his birth certificate states … (the war was a melting pot … throwing them together at the steel works). He now lives in Robin Hood's Bay, North Yorkshire. He's in a few writing groups … (Natalie keeps the Whitby Library Writing Group blog up to date … it's too tricky for John). He sticks to sonnets, as the form exercises some control of his worst excesses. They pile up … the excesses … He likes anthologies … he enjoys the company … (and there's safety in numbers …).
E: johntunaley@yahoo.co.uk

RULES FOR MANCUNIANS

They looked feasible, practical, sane and
familiar. My own tribe, (working class ...
... Mancunian), might well recognise them.
I mean 'The Seven Maori Practices ...

'Show a respect for people', (for even
City fans are human). 'Be seen', (the ... 'thought
I'd better come and show my face' approach).
'Look, listen, speak' ... (in that order. Quite a
tall one for our lot, we could do better).

'Host ... be generous' ...(all those aunts bringing
plate after piled plate!). 'Be cautious' ... (be alert
for the smell of rats...see 'look, listen, speak')
'Don't trample on folks Mana' ... (well... perish the thought).
'Don't flaunt your knowledge ... (for no-one loves a smart-ass)...

Tanja Ajtic
CANADA / SERBIA

Tanja studied at the Faculty of Philology, Department of Serbian Language and Literature in Belgrade. She then worked in administrative affairs at the Federal Court until 2002 when she moved to Canada. Her poems and stories have been translated into Serbian, English, Croatian, Bosnian, Bulgarian, Iraqi and Bengali, and published in more than 160 collections, anthologies, e-books and magazines worldwide. Her book *Outlines of Love* was exhibited at the 2018 Book Fair in Belgrade, as well as at the 2019 Book Salon in Toronto. Amongst many other international awards, she is among the thirty best writers for 2020 by the Association of Writers of Australia.
E: tajtic@gmail.com
FB: @tanja.ajtic

ROOTS

There was a mill and
a tailor's shop of the city
family in Lika.
There was one river
and enmity between
the villages,
each from its own coast.
There was one big one a tribe
that was killed in the war
and only one family survived
who set out on a journey
for Belgrade.
From two enemy villages
two young men and women
stared at each other
and started a family,
big, love has won.
They were all mine, and now they are gone.
There is no one, I am alone.
Sometimes I can smell the orange
being heated on the furnace.
Sometimes I see wheat
in a wreath with a lighted candle
for Serbian Christmas.
Sometimes I feel holy water
when I cross myself
with three fingers
and I finish the prayer in my heart.
Sometimes I feel blood and hear
screams and see fire,
I see villages and towns in Lika
and then everything disappears.
And I have to write,
to feel and think...
How did I lose them all during my life
and before my life?

TRADITION

Oh, Lika is far away now, Montenegro and Serbia,
my roots are far away
where I belong.
Here I wear traditional shoes and a vest
and play a folk dance
sometimes
to feel, to remember my ancestors.
But I write ... I write easily ...
I receive energy from the universe,
from my roots, at great distances.
And it always is.
It is not me who writes it, it is my great-grandparents
from the Balkans.
We are always in a relationship, unbreakable, bloody.
That is what the Serbian woman sings in me,
she also writes a picture
from a small country, proud.
I do not forget the origin,
it is with me
in every breath and exhalation
in the heart,
the soul
because that's how I was traditionally brought up.

My country is sad
in eternal damnation
that there is no primordial happiness
and that is why I carry sorrow,
always and when I laugh
and I am happy,
there is some sadness indescribable
in my eyes.
But poem and stories, pictures are not.
I resist.
Because my country knows how to sing
and to rejoice, to dance,
my Balkan country.

I am Serbian and
I like to tilt my hat
and wink and smile shifty,
I can do that well

even if my eyes are wet
with sadness from my unhappy
generations.

Aminath Neena
MALDIVES

Aminath has an MA TESOL from the University of Nottingham, and is an English lecturer from the picturesque archipelago nation of the Maldives. An avid lover of words, poetry is a hobby closest to her heart. Her poems usually revolve around themes such as love, relationships, spirituality, society, and global issues. Her poems are published or are forthcoming in a range of international platforms like the *Trouvaille Review, Spill words, The Poet Magazine, Fiddles & Scribbles, Muddy River Poetry Review*, *Imspired magazine, Continue the voice magazine* and *Borderless Journal*. Her poems have also been nested in some anthologies like *Eccentric Orbits* by Dimensionfold publishing and *Poetica 2 and 3* of Clarendon House publications and many such others. Her bio is featured in the *Who's Who of Emerging Writers 2020 and 2021*, published by Sweetycat Press Publications. She believes her writings to be a reflection of her thoughts, her feelings, and her life.
E: aminathneenahanyf@gmail.com
FB: @aminath.neena

BRAVE HEART

She saw him,
The nimble toddy man,
"Brave heart"
They called him
He was the champion of the tribe

Oh! He was the brewer
of the greatest dream
approaching as a light beam
In the midnight sky

And in front of her,
he stopped for a while
Lovingly watching the poised Venus
waving to him from beneath
the murky Sirius

with her delicately framed emerald coils
nourished by the succulent soils
Upon which martyrs and heroes

Stamped their footsteps
Dipped in sacred blood
that prevailed over generations

Ever faithful, ever loving
she gestated humming
a melodious aubade
when he started mounting her
gliding higher and higher

and together, she and he
they swayed with the turbulent breeze
Unaware of the tribal creed
Unaccustomed to the extent of viciousness
of them lot, the ruthless breed

with conflict and greed
and grievances untamed
of a history sustained
In jigsaw puzzles
and noble as he was,

Brave heart, he forgave them all
every single one of them foes

So, with his heart
Murmuring Kosher tales
of once upon a prosperous homeland
He, the noble cavalry man
Worked on the meticulous details

of wrapping her curls tight
Before the first streak of daylight
of every single morn

to collect the sweet brew
For which, the conch they blew

to nourish his people
the old, the weary, the homeless,
the child and the aimless
friend or foe no matter
though he could hear the chatter
of the ruthless ungrateful fodder

at the battle of the warlord
for which some were paid in gold

Light as a feather
he kept working on her curls
with silent gratitude
and his teardrops glistened
while tying and untying
the loosened braids

when lips touching his ear
softly, she whispered,

'Tell me your dreams'

And way down below the turf
that fateful dawn
he could see the bronzed silver dwarf
of the squadron march
aiming straight at his heart
He blinked and the toddy fell apart

all hell broke loose

when his head fit the noose

And that day in the island

with her braids loose once again
the coconut palm, she wept
yearning for his nimble touch again
wanting for her champion to rise
craving for liberty
and with each teardrop that she shed
the soil beneath her trembled
and bled

Claudia Hardt
BAHRAIN / GERMANY

A PR & Communications Specialist, Claudia has lived and worked in Europe, Asia and the Middle East. Inspired by the rich culture, heritage and natural beauty of Bahrain, her writing and poetry focuses on the tradition of pearl diving and the pearl. She has contributed to several books, including *More of My Beautiful Bahrain* and *Poetic Bahrain*. Claudia also regularly uses her passion for adventure trips and photography to create travel stories and columns which have been published in places such as Malaysia, Hong Kong, Cyprus, Bahrain, UAE and Germany.
E: claudiahardt@hotmail.de

MY DEEP BLUE SEA

My deep blue sea
You are my passion and devotion,
My imagination and emotion,
You are my harbour,
My home, where my soul finds rest,
On the edge of the ocean's breast.

My deep blue sea
You surround me with darkness and light,
You give me hope and a lustrous sight,
You are my harbour,
My home, where nothing can set us apart
In this wonderful deep sea world of art.

My deep blue sea
Your waves, all around, wrap me in peace,
Your gentle waves keep my heart at ease,
You are my harbour,
My home, where silence speaks a million words,
Unique and mystic, my wonderful world.

My deep blue sea
You are my one, my secret friend,
My companion to the end,
My deepest, dearest love,
You are my harbour,
And my only homeland.

Always and forever,
Gumasha

Chester Civelli
SWITZERLAND

Chester is a poet and singer-songwriter. He has released two self-published poetry books: *Encre & Nuages* and *Mysticismes,* and has had poems featured in various webzines and magazines. He is currently working on the release of a poetry anthology proceeding from an online monthly event he held in 2021.
E: chester.civelli@gmail.com
FB: @PoetryReadingOnline
Instagram: @poetry_reading_online
YouTube: @Poetry Reading Online

ANTHEM

Hear the voices
Singing together
On the first of August

It's been centuries
Four
Became
Twenty-six
And one
And four as well

Words they don't understand
They don't know where they come from

Standing
Hand on the heart
Head high
Eyes (half) closed

And I remain seated ...

Fireworks in the sky
Wonders in the brains
Terror in the branches
But it's only once a year right

Crowds gathering
On the shores of the lakes
On the boats
On the balconies

And I watch them from afar...

*

Is that pride?
Is that pride?
What is pride
When it comes to a country?
        to "your" country?

*

It's all a matter of luck
And luck
What is it?

"invisible, insignificant, and meaningless
Of no use"1

When you think about it
Everywhere is beautiful
Everywhere is paradise
Everywhere where there's life
Everywhere where there's love

When you think about it
Everywhere is beautiful
It's hate
And hatred and jealousy and pride and war
That's what makes it ugly

So
Instead of singing
A song I don't know
For a drawing
On a piece of paper
– you don't see frontiers
from space do you? –
I remained seated
And reflected on
How lucky I am

Prof. Ron Roman
SOUTH KOREA

Associate Professor of English (Ret'd), ESL, and Humanities Ron taught with the University of Maryland Global Campus (UMGC) all over the Pacific since January 1996. He studied writing (both fiction and creative) for his third graduate degree (Humanities) from Wesleyan University. He retired from full-time employ (August 2009), and as adjunct (May 2020). Hobbies include jogging, hiking, camping, weightlifting, roller-coasters, and his beloved 1968 Rambler American antique auto for which he received Third Prize in the Hemmings (*Motor News*) National Antique Auto Show in Bennington, Vermont in August 1994, shortly before returning overseas. (The Rambler is currently under restoration.) He has written extensive travel, academic, and political op-ed articles for regional, national and international publications. His thriller novel *Of Ashes and Dust* is scheduled to be released in the fall of 2022 by Addison-Highsmith (imprint). Currently he resides in Pyeongtaek, South Korea, with his wife, writes in miscellaneous genres, and works part-time counselling US military retirees and spouses on American military installations.
E: ron_g_roman@hotmail.com

REBIRTH AT SAGES RAVINE

Whitewater churning over the rockface,
Tumbling over the falls at a furious pace.
This sacred spot forever speaks to the essence of the heart,
Bathing in Nature's beauty, and submerged in her intricate art.

Green ferns languishingly droop over the hidden ravine,
Nary a ray of noon sunlight peeks through to be seen,
Winds whistle overhead through swaying fir tree tops,
Cawing of crows and raucousness of jays seemingly never stops.

Icy spray from deep inside the roaring gorge kisses and rejuvenates naked skin,
Creating the realization that here life-awakening epiphany has yet always been.
For when under the falls of Sages Ravine each time you're reborn,
Ensconced by Nature's pulsating Glory, powerful, resilient, and never forlorn.

Rozalia Aleksandrova
BULGARIA

Rozalia was born in the magical Rhodope Mountains, the cradle of Orpheus, and now lives in Plovdiv, one of Europe's oldest settlements. She is the author of 11 poetry books: *The House of My Soul* (2000), *Shining Body* (2003), *The Mystery of the Road* (2005), *The Eyes of the Wind* (2007), *Parable of the key* (2008), *The Conversation between Pigeons* (2010), *Sacral* (2013), *The Real Life of Feelings* (2015), *Pomegranate from Narrow* (2016), *Brushy* (2017), and *Everything I did not say* (2019). Editor and compiler of over ten literary almanacs, collections and anthologies, she is a member of the Union of Bulgarian Writers. In March 2006 she created a poetic-intellectual association Quantum and Friends for the promotion of quantum poetry in civil society. She is initiator and organizer of the International Festival of Poetry 'Spirituality Without Borders' from 2015, which, for seven consecutive years, has brought together poets from Bulgaria, Europe and the world in an atmosphere of tolerance, friendship and the love of human speech. Every year the Festival publishes a poetry almanac, with which the participating poets present themselves to the Plovdiv and foreign audiences. The Festival also participates in joint initiatives with other festivals in Bulgaria and abroad including 'Festiwal poezji slowianskiej' (London), 'Festiwal poezji slowianskiej' (Czechowice-Dziedzice, Polska), 'Festival of Poetry' (Turkey), and others, and in Plovdiv: the International Festival Days of Thracian Culture.
E: rozalia54@yahoo.com
FB: @РозалияАлександрова

AND AFTER

Birds that leave at night
in white nameless fields,
are celestial guests
who have stopped the cosmos
in the weekday cry of being.
The ancient Bulgarian sword and above
He gathers
the Warriors of the Spirit.
Who
is created
to love,
even if he leaves
does not die.

Zorica Bajin Đukanović
SERBIA

Zorica graduated from the Faculty of Philology of Belgrade University, the Department of Yugoslav Literature. She writes poetry, prose and literature for the young, and has published a total of 17 books including the collections of poetry *Blood Clot* (1994) and *Lining* (1999), the short story collections *Hotel Philosopher* (2003) and *Said King Of Sunshades* (2009) and the following collections of poetry for young people: *Wizard* (1999), *Tiny Box For A Firefly* (2010), *Summer Day* (2014) and *Brief Love Poems* (2017). Her poetry and prose have been translated into Russian, English, Dutch, Rumanian, Ruthenian and Macedonian, and her work has been featured in 60 anthologies, chrestomathies, textbooks and readers. She lives and works in Belgrade as a freelance artist.
E: poemleto@gmail.com

LJUBICA
Translated from the Serbian original by Novica Petrovic

She waits
puzzled that death
cares not about her death
her soul has gone full circle
and now everything is unravelling
from the end to the beginning
so now she is lit again
by the early light

We steal upon her
pagan children
Hansel and Gretel
from the fairy tales she used to read to us
we ask he about her name
silence
about love
muteness
about the home and what we are to her
nothing

We lean over her
the distant contours
of her face spread across ours
immeasurably distant
from the bristling wire
in front of which it was
I will concerning tomorrow morning
I won't concerning disappearing

Then the thought strikes us
and who are you what are you
her eyes light up
in front of the last
memory not erased
that tape of Krapp's
that one cross of hers
was replaced by another
and some distant name
so she enunciates the name of her faith
trembling so
as if naked for the first time

ANNA'S LETTER, A LETTER TO ANNA
For Marko Tomaš
Translated from the Serbian original by Novica Petrovic

When it arrived
it was inside another letter
like a pit like a germ
it was delivered into my hands
ticking like an explosive device
I didn't know what to do with it
so I put it aside
in a secret compartment of the secretary desk
the way Andrić did with the money
saved for encroaching destitution
it wasn't addressed to me
so why did that stray shrapnel
go straight for me
then I poked
through the ashes of photos
and finally saw you
on the bank of the Sava in the clothes of a boy
you shone
this photo is a bang
why didn't you stay on that bank
everything was there
and everything was yours

In May I looked at the sky
and was puzzled that
the roof of our house was gone
we are still three little pigs
caught by a storm
you enter the city on a white horse
I rub my eyes
I hear shots being fired
and conclude that this
is not a performance by Marina
you are real
more real than everything real
a star is on your forehead
not on your stomach
you have a bob haircut
created for you by epidemic typhus
you ate moss and grass

and now your liver is tattered
why didn't you stay on that bank
he too is a warrior a highlander
you don't know anything about his country
whether it is smart
to couple with so much that's unknown
I know you'd say we'll see how you fare
comrades from the highlands
chill watermelons in bidets
and prepare polenta for the new holidays
abundance is a source of headache and dizziness

Your father Joseph without brothers
was a stationmaster
you had a free ticket
to the end of every railway
you could have lived in Greenland
but no you set off
into the mystery of those woods
and when you raved in the grip of fever
you only saw the blue
you stand on the diving board
shining like Hedy Lamarr
I take a deep breath
and wait to see that jump
underwater I hear
you're a Polack
hell no I'm no Polack
Yugoslav
there's no ... slav of yours here
just Polack
look what they've done
to our song Ma

Volkan Hacıoğlu
TURKEY

Volkan received Bachelor of Arts in 2000, and Master of Arts in 2003 and a Ph.D. In 2010, and lectures courses on Aesthetics at Nazim Hikmet Academy. His poems, essays on poetry, and poetry translations appeared in various international and national journals and magazines. He has eight books of poetry published, and won several international poetry awards. He was the-editor-in-chief of the international multilingual magazine *Rosetta World Literatura*. His books include: *Duvarlarda Gözlerim Üşüyor* (2006), *Dansa Kaldırılmayan Kadın* (2010), *Ahenk Kapısı* (2013), *Budapeşte Radyosu* (2016), *Şehri Terk Eden Hayalet* (2017), *Doğu Hindistan Kumpanyası* (2017), *Zerdüşt ve Kırlangıç* (2018), *Unutulmuş Aryalar* (2019); *şiir çevirileri: Anarşinin Maskesi,* (Percy Bysshe Shelley, 2010); *Neşideler,* (Behruz Kia, 2013); *Seçilmiş Şiirler,* (Ralph Waldo Emerson, 2016); *Şiirler,* (Ralph Hodgson, 2016); *deneme-inceleme: Köşeli Parantez* (Sanat ve Edebiyat Yazıları 2016) and *Poetik Meditasyonlar* (2018).
E: volkan_hacioglu@yahoo.com
W: www.volkanhacioglu.wixsite.com/thepoet
FB: @616784647
Instagram: @volkan_hacioglu
Twitter: @volkanthepoet

ON REMEMBRANCE OF MY FIRST POEM THAT HAS BEEN LOST

On a Byzantine day of days
We've been terribly caught
By a King Lear rain—
Whilst crossing the boulevard street
Over the shadow of old Drama Theatre.

And the sun was an utmost Fool
At the continental shelf of Love
The Fates were preening through darkness
With a vast fan of time in their hand.

I might have been eight or ten years
Of old at that time as getting across
Under teeming rain and soaking wet
My father suddenly called out to me:—

"Don't dare to be a poet like me!"
And when I asked why?—he smiled
With sorrow and said: "You see
How miserable we have been through … "

It was the moment I decided to be a poet
And the name of my first poem that is lost
Remained in my mind: "Eyes Under the Rain,"
On a King Lear day of days—
Over the curtain of old Drama Theatre.

Hussein Habasch
KURDISTAN / GERMANY

Hussein is a poet from Afrin, Kurdistan. He currently lives in Bonn, Germany. His poems have been translated into English, German, Spanish, French, Chinese, Turkish, Persian, Albanian, Uzbek, Russian, Italian, Bulgarian, Lithuanian, Hungarian, Macedonian, Serbian, Polish and Romanian, and has had his poetry published in a large number of international anthologies. His books include: *Drowning in Roses, Fugitives across Evros River, Higher than Desire and more Delicious than the Gazelle's Flank, Delusions to Salim Barakat, A Flying Angel, No pasarán* (in Spanish), *Copaci Cu Chef* (in Romanian), *Dos Árboles and Tiempos de Guerra* (in Spanish), *Fever of Quince* (in Kurdish), *Peace for Afrin, peace for Kurdistan* (in English and Spanish), *The Red Snow* (in Chinese), *Dead arguing in the corridors* (in Arabic) and *Drunken trees* (in Kurdish). He participated in many international festivals of poetry including: Colombia, Nicaragua, France, Puerto Rico, Mexico, Germany, Romania, Lithuania, Morocco, Ecuador, El Salvador, Kosovo, Macedonia, Costa Rica, Slovenia, China, Taiwan and New York City.
E: habasch70@hotmail.com
FB: @hussein.habasch

Birînek navê wê EFRÎN e

Ez ê dilê xwe ji kambaxiya
ku bi salan zirarê pê dike rizgar bikim
û ji lekeyên xemginiya tarî û êşa şîn, baqij bikim.
Ez ê qalikên ziwa ji ser dîwarê wî rêş bikim
û qujmirandinên kûr yên
ku li ser rûyê wî derketine, dûz bikim.
Ez ê goştê mirî jê bibirim
û dohnê ku di rehên wî de kom bûye, bikşînim.
Erê, ez ê her tiştî serrast bikim,
lê tenê ezê birînek kûr ku herroj têde mezin dibe, bihêlim!
Navê wê birînê jî EFRÎN e.
Ez tukesî nahêlim ku bi wê bilîze, xwe jê nêzîk bike,
Yan jî wê derman bike.
Na, ez nahêlim!
Ew birîna dilê min e, tenê ya dilê min e
û pê lêdanên dilê min serrast dibin!
û ji bo wê tenê ez dijîm û sax dibim.

A WOUND CALLED AFRIN
Translated by Azad Akkash

I shall restore my heart
from the devastation it received through the years.
I shall remove the dark stains of sadness,
the blue bruises of pain.
From its walls, I shall remove the dry crusts
and the deep wrinkles that appeared on its skin.
I shall remove the decaying flesh,
the fat built-up in its arteries.
Yet, I am keeping a single deep wound
that keeps growing in my heart,
a wound called Afrin!
I shall never let anybody mess with it,
to come close to it,
or to try to heal it.
It is the wound of my heart alone.
With it, my heart beats get regulated.
For its sake, my heart lives.

NOTE: Afrin is my city occupied by the Turkish army and the extremist Syrian Islamic opposition gangs since 2018. Every day, various types of violations against the Kurds occur, including killing, arrest, kidnapping, robbery and theft.

Weke Kurdekî ku ji serhishkiya xwe hez bike!

Ez ji van ciyayên asê
û ji van cemên ku bi çogên sist digihînin dawiya habûna xwe, hez
dikim.
Ez ji van kevirên ku serhiskiyê, di kela germbûna havînê de, bi tîna
rokê re dikin,
hez dikim.
Ez ji vê axa ku rengê wê weke rengê lasê min e
û vê xaka ku ew ji berî hemû tishtan dilê min e, hez dikim.
Ez ji vê toza ku ew kila çavên min e
Û ji vî bayê ku ew dermanê cegera min e, hez dikim.
Ez ji van kizwanên bejin kin
û ji van guvîjên bêhnxweş, hez dikim.
Ez ji van sorbelanan û stiriyên wan,
û ji van zeytûnan û ji bîranînên wan, hez dikim.
Ez ji vî qamîşê zirav yê ku herdem li ser kenara çem distire
û ji vê gola tarî ku têde beq bê vehes diqîrin, hez dikim.
Ez ji van kulîlkên mêst yên spî weke dilê min
û van ganguliyên ku biratiya xwîna min dikin, hez dikim
Ez ji van malên axî
û ji van konên ku weke alan li derdorên gundên jibîrkirî liba dibin, hez
dikim
Ez ji van rezên comerd ku tirî û meyê didin me
û ji van guliyên zer yên gênim ku nan û xwarinê didin me, hez dikim.
Ez ji van tîtîyên ku bixwe serbilind
û ji van sîsirkên ku herdem di tariyê fît dikin, hez dikim.
Ez ji welatê xwe
Ji binî ta serî
û ji serî ta binî, hez dikim,
hez dikim weke Kurdekî ku ji serhishkiya xwe hez bike,
hez dikim.

AS A KURD WOULD LOVE HIS STUBBORNNESS!
Translated by Azad Akkash

I love these rugged mountains
and these slender rivers
with wobbly knees pouring into their charnel house.
I love these stones that defy sunrays
in the midsummer heat
and the frosty cold in midwinter chills.
I love this soil that resembles my body
and this land that foremost means the heart.
I love this dust, a coal for my eyes it is,
and this air, a balm for my lungs it is.
I love this skimpy terebinth
and the fragrant hawthorn.
I love cacti and its thorns,
olives and its yearnings.
I love this thin reed that serenades all the time
on the river bank,
this dark swamp where frogs continuously croak.
I love the daisy flower that resembles the whiteness
of my heart,
and these tulips that fraternize with my blood.
I love these mud houses
and these tents, fluttering on the outskirts of
forgotten villages.
I love this generous vine, the bequeather of grapes
and wine.
I love these yellow grain spikes, the bequeather of food
and bread.
I love these swaggering kite birds,
and these cicadas, continuously singing.
I love my land
from top to bottom
and from bottom to top,
just as a Kurd would love his stubbornness!

Tessa Thomson
ENGLAND

Tessa was always able to tell good stories, but it was only when she reached her septuagenarian era did she put those stories into verse. Her first collection of poems, *Finding my Voice* was published in March 2021. Her poems are reflective, often biographical and sometimes spiritual. Many demonstrate a resilience to overcome life's many knocks; tragedies that for some might have proved impossible to conquer.
E: tessathomson1@gmail.com

WE ALL MATTER

Do I matter? Am I thinking, that I am just a spare,
Someone left to fill the space to show them all you care.
Do I matter? Is it standing by and waiting for my turn,
Amidst the others of my kind that leads to such concern.

Does it matter that my skin is white or black or even old.
As long as you can change the facts and somehow break the mould.
Can't you see it's in our history. It's our past we must uphold.
But our future is the change we'll make, the future is our goal.

It's our goal to be resilient not to fear the tides of change.
To embrace the difference in our lives so hearts can rearrange,
Their attitude to others whose lives seem set to fail,
Because the colour of their skin belies the ship they sail.

We are *Allsorts* in a see-through bag, a mixture all enclosed,
In a world that wants to set apart each tribe and recompose,
The world into a worsening state by keeping tribes apart,
Not letting all from everywhere be offered the same start.

We are hindered by the past, by the mores of long ago.
We are shackled to what seemed right then, unable to let go.
We have moved to a position, we have made enormous strides.
But we linger on in no-man's land, in ignorance abide.

It's not enough to bend a knee, to raise a tightened fist.
But try instead to change the minds of those who still insist,
That he is not my brother, she is not like me.
In this one world we all exist and somehow must agree.

David A Banks
ENGLAND

David lives in a seaside town on the north east coast of England. His first career was in telecommunications after which he taught, researched and published in the higher education sector. The latter career provided opportunities to live and/or work in the UK, Singapore, New Zealand, Hong Kong, Australia and the US. Now retired, his pursuits include gardening, wood and leather working and writing poetry and short plays.
E: traveldab@gmail.com

PERCEPTIONS

If you walk in the blood red deserts of Australia
you will sometimes see
marks in the rocky ground
that remind you of ripples on a beach.

For a person of science this is perfectly explicable,
and should such a person take the time to share their wisdom
with a native of this arid land
they would explain how this desert was once the bed of a shallow sea
that over millennia slowly rose above the water
until eventually it formed the surface of this land
and the ripples that you see
once marked that ancient sea bed.

The native of that land would probably smile politely
and nod their heads.

When they later relate this tale to their kin
there will be some laughter and
one of the elders will explain to the children
the true story of how the great ancestor lizard shaped the land
and left its claw marks in the rock.

They will tell their gathered children
and their children's future children
and their forefathers
and their forefathers forefathers,
who will all be present at the meeting,
how foolish it seems that the scientist visitor
can believe in mountains rising from the sea
and yet not understand how we really exist
in a world populated by all that live,
have lived and are yet to live.

Bhuwan Thapaliya
NEPAL

Bhuwan is the author of four poetry collections *Safa Tempo: Poems New and Selected, Our Nepal, Our Pride, Rhythm of the Heart* and *Verses from the Himalayas*, and is currently working on his latest collection *The Marching Millions*. He has read his poetry and attended seminars in venues around the world including: South Korea, the USA, Thailand, Cambodia, and Nepal, and his work has been widely published in leading literary journals, newspapers and periodicals such as *Kritya, The Foundling Review, ApekshaNews, Strong Verse, Counercurrents.org, myrepublica, The Kashmir Pulse, Taj Mahal Review, Nuveine Magazine, Poetry Life and Times, Ponder Savant, VOICES(Education Project), The Vallance Review, Longfellow Literary Project, Poets Against the War* and others. His poetry has also been published in CDs and books including: *The New Pleiades Anthology of Poetry, Tonight: An Anthology of World Love Poetry and The Strand Book of International Poets 2010,* and many more.
E: nepalipoet@yahoo.com

RICKETY CHAIR

Every morning my father stands on one foot,
arms raised in Surya Namaskar above his head
offering prayers to a solar deity, fully absorbed
within himself for half an hour in the rooftop,
and then sits down in a rickety chair
nearby his desultory guest,
an amiable serene cat and smiles looking
at the sunlight streaming through flowers.
Shiny plants, attired in colourful earthen pots
shades of white and blue, red and brown,
stretches out from one end to the other.
A riot of colours in the myriad flowers
appeases his mind and eyes.
My father lives a routine life like he wants to
but he has strong connections to certain things.
One such thing is his rickety chair.
Over the years it has rusted completely
but he thinks it looks more attractive now.
It's been on the rooftop for over 20 years now.
Father, the chair is too old and cranky.
Let me replace it for you, every alternate day I shout.
"I admit that over the years the colours have erased a bit
but I feel that's what gives it a more character, more charisma.
I don't need a new chair," looking straight in my eyes
he always shrinks my requests.
"Come and sit here and in just a minute it will
transport you into a whole new world,
far from the frenzied turbulence
of the bustling metropolis,
stirring and serene," he whispered in my ear
earlier today when I went up to give him
a cup of masala tea.
I just smiled and told myself,
no, I can't lean back in the rickety chair
and conjure my mind and spread my arms
to hug the world around me.
I may land painfully on my hip.
"It's alright my son," my father said sensing my dilemma.
Nonetheless, to appreciate and thank the chair
that has brought me this far. I decided to sit in the chair.
"Close your eyes, take a deep breath
and enjoy the journey my son," he said with a big grin on his face.

Morning air embroidered with his smiles created senses
that evoked the beauty of an impending era.
"We don't need a new chair.
This chair is very comfortable," I told my father.
He smiled.
We both smiled
as the immigrants in a new city
they soon will be embracing as their own.

William Khalipwina Mpina
MALAWI

William is a poet, fiction writer, essayist, editor, economist and teacher. His writing reflects on the mundane and the everyday experiences. Many of his works appear in online international literary magazines such as *Kalahari Review, Literary Shanghai, Writers Space Africa, African writer, Nthanda review, Scribble Publication, Atunis Galaxy Poetry, Poetica* and *Expound Magazine*; and in over ten local anthologies. A co-editor of *Walking the Battlefield* and *Tilembe Newsletter* of Malawi Union of Academic and Non-fiction Authors, Mpina has contributed verses in international anthologies such as *Lockdown 2020, On the Road, A New World: Rethinking our lives post pandemic, Writing Robotics: Africa versus Asia, Christmas* and others. His books include *Princess from the Moon* (2020), *Shattered Dreams* (2019), *Blood Suckers* (2019), *Shadows of Death and other poems* (2016), *Namayeni* (2009), and *Njiru* (2003).
E: williammpina3@gmail.com
FB: @Khalipwina.Mpina
Twitter: @William.Mpina

LET ME BE WHO I AM

They say I am not who I am
Because they are who they are
They are serious I must not be
Who I am when they are who they are
Why? My people are warriors
My people know how to fight with their teeth
And they are called *alhomwe*,
A clan which knows how to bite
They can but not lose a fight
I am a *Lhomwe*, and they know I am
I cannot be somebody else
I come from the land of the *Lhomwe*
I am loose but not free
Let me be who I am
Let me be where I want to be

WHO ARE THEY?

They ask me to tell them the truth
I do not have the truth they want
I have the truth about myself and my race
The black race, the despicable race
The truth is I hunt and eat mice
I drink sweet brew called *thobwa*
Stored in pots hidden under trees of *mpoza*
The tree of spirits, the spirits of rain
I dance *tchopa*, the rain dance
I have a god called *chisumphi*
The creator of the earth and man
And I have several wives to please my peace
Nephews and nieces to protect my territory
I am fortified. My freedom is unchained
I am who I am. Now tell me: who are they
To ask me of what they will not understand?

P. J. Reed
ENGLAND

P.J writes the *Richard Radcliffe Paranormal Investigations* series and is the editor and chief paranormal investigator for the *Exmoor Noir* newsletter. She has written a series of poetry collections including the *Haiku Seasons* series - *Haiku Yellow, Haiku Gold, Haiku Summer*, and *Haiku Ice,* as well as a collection entitled *Simply Senryu*, featuring Flicker and Pandemica. Her monologues, both Comic and Dark, have been performed in theatres across Britain, and are available to download from Smiths Scripts.

E: pjreedwriting@gmail.com
W: pjreedwriting.wixsite.com/poetry
Instagram @pjreedwriter
Twitter @PJReed_author

MY CULTURE

My culture is white English
with a maternal slice of Welsh.
While my red-headed late father
sailed over with the Vikings,
pillaged, enslaved, and stayed –
a thousand years of Englishness.
A life lived in unending shades,
of bland, bleached monotony,
I looked longingly to the east,
to vibrant Chinese dragons
or fiery Japanese Samurai,
as I ate my Devonshire scones.
I spread cream on first, of course,
I'm not a culinary criminal,
but a Deoxyribonucleic acid test
revealed an unexpected twist-
I am a ginger, Spanish Viking,
by way of India.

George David
ROMANIA

George has been writing both poetry and fiction for more than 40 years. He debuted with the poetry book *The Mountain of Sounds* (1990), followed by several others: *Deliricatesses & Spleendors* (2015), *Songbook* (2018) and *Photo with a Missing Angel* (2018). He has also published prose, including: *At Foreigners – Their Secret Lives* (2017, 2020), and the novel *The Black Plague. The Word Traders* (2020), a fourteenth-century fiction frequently reminding us about the ongoing COVID 19 pandemic.
E: george.g.david@gmail.com
FB: George.G.David1957

WASTED SONG

soldier with no homeland
and therefore, with no glory,
with no brave captain,
but also, with no rear,
with no loved ones
waiting for him at home,
with no shadow
to harden some time
in a statue

SAD LULLABY SONG

once born from your placenta, mother,
I have passed into another one.
the pure baby who I used to be right after my birth
has been irremediably lost today

going through thousands of painful births,
this sphere no longer belongs to me.
under its heavy shadow I tighten my neck
trying to escape its foreign borders

I give birth to myself, but I also die moment by moment,
endowed with shards of future and past.
I always slip hurry-scurry from a placenta to another placenta,
from that of a mother to the one made of dust

ANOTHER SAD LULLABY SONG

mother with a thousand of eyes,
with a thousand of reptilian arms
not with nails ending up, but Cyclops
with electric eye pupils

today you give birth to some eyelid of mine,
tomorrow you'll add me even a hand
and while you're delivering me, you grind me,
relentless machine!

mom, mechanical, heart-breaking mom!
why do you stop me from conceiving myself?
don't be afraid, don't be afraid, mom,
my wing belongs to you, mom
and with it I am inner-chaining
myself into you!

Irma Kurti
ITALY / ALBANIA

Irma is an Albanian poet, writer, lyricist, journalist, and translator, and a naturalized Italian. She has been writing since she was a child and has published 22 books in Albanian, 15 in Italian and 4 in English. She has also written about 150 lyrics for adults and children, in both Italian and English. All her books are dedicated to the memory of her beloved parents Hasan Kurti and Sherife Mezini, who supported and encouraged every step of her literary path. Kurti has won numerous literary prizes and awards in Italy and Italian Switzerland, and has been awarded the Universum Donna International Prize IX Edition 2013 for Literature, and the lifetime nomination of Ambassador of Peace by the University of Peace of Italian Switzerland. In 2020, she received the title of Honorary President of WikiPoesia, the *Encyclopaedia of Poetry*. In 2021, she was awarded the title Liria (Freedom) by the Arbëreshë Community in Italy.

E: kurtial@yahoo.com
FB: @IrmaKurtiAutore
Instagram: @irma.kurti

IN THE MOTHER TONGUE

When fatigue takes root in my body
and darkness descends on the trees,
it happens often that in my mother tongue
I utter a whole sentence unintentionally.

When I roam in the dim world of dreams,
sometimes I'm choked by anxiety and fear,
I don't ask for help in a foreign language,
a single word of my language saves me.

In those precise moments I do not realize:
no one understands what I've pronounced,
because it so naturally flows from my soul
as among the rocks a stream goes quietly.

THIS HOUSE IS NOT SOLD
To my house in Tirana

This house cannot be sold, there sleep
and wake up thousands of memories,
like colourless crumbs flicker in the air
the words that we left, all our dreams.

The corridor narrowed from solitude
with the steps of my mother was filled,
the comings and goings of my parents
resonate there as a divine symphony.

In the living room the sofas are rotten,
this one – old and decaying may seem,
but my father often leaned on it,
it keeps his presence even now vivid.

It still felt of the smell of hot coffee
two steps away, in a very small annex,
I don't compare it with the best aromas
vended everywhere in the shops today.

The huge picture hanging on the wall
representing a big home on an island,
portrays my desire to live somewhere
with all my family, in a better world.

The memoirs give it a great value,
make it dear, not regarding the price,
but for my heart and for my feelings.
It's not sold, it's not bought – the house!

THE WALLS DON'T BELONG TO ME

This magical sunset fixes snowflakes
as they fall confused and disorderly,
falling in love with each one of them.

I stay motionless in front of my house,
I don't feel any desire to enter,
to be wrapped in its oppressive heat.

Tonight the walls don't belong to me
I am one with this white landscape,
it doesn't let go, it keeps me hostage.

The snow melts, as part of the show,
thousands of crystals on my shoulders
just like infinite kisses given by love.

My soul is mutated into a light feather,
with snowflakes it wanders in the air,
I cannot escape from it; I have to wait.

And then, together turn home.

Bill Cox
SCOTLAND

Bill was born and bred in 'the Granite City' of Aberdeen, where he still lives along with his partner Hilary, and their grown-up baby daughter Catherine. Bill enjoyed creative writing when at school, but as the cliché goes; life got in the way and it was only in his forties, after taking an online course, that he returned to his teenage passion. He now writes for the sheer enjoyment of it, which is just as well as no-one seems willing to pay him to do it. He dabbles mainly in poetry and short fiction, as he hasn't built up the stamina yet to write anything longer. One day, though, he plans to gather his strength and write a book that will set the publishing world alight. In the meantime he satisfies himself with composing bawdy limericks in his head.

E: malphesius@yahoo.com
W: www.northeastnotesblog.wordpress.com

JOCK TAMSON'S BAIRNS

In this country of lochs and mountain cairns,
We understand we're all Jock Tamson's bairns.
Come hither, we'll welcome you with open arms,
And demonstrate all our nations' charms.

It may be you think you know us well already,
The picture in your minds-eye is perhaps quite steady.
Is it ... ?
Playing the bagpipes, Highland dancing,
Chasing haggis, through purple heather prancing.
Swigging whisky by the bottle,
David Hume is our Aristotle.
Highland games, tossing the caber,
We've got the English for a neighbour.
Men in kilts, tartan fabric galore,
The Loch Ness monster swimming ashore.

Now, most of these traits are caricatures,
Not our normal behaviours, to be sure!
While in every cliché, there's a hint of the true,
In actual fact, we're just much like you.
So do yourself a favour, come for a stay,
And see the real Scotland, each and every day.

Dr. Ana Stjelja
SERBIA

Ana graduated from the Faculty of Philology from the Turkish Language and Literature Department. In 2009 she earned a Master's Degree in Sufism, and in 2012 obtained her PhD in Serbian Literature (*with the thesis on the life and work of one of the first Serbian women writers and world travellers Jelena J. Dimitrijević*). She is a poet, writer, translator, journalist, researcher and editor, and has published more than 30 books of different literary genres. She is the Editor-in-chief of the *Alia Mundi* magazine for cultural diversity, and the online literary magazine *Enheduana*. She is also the founder and the editor of the *Eastern Pearl* - a web portal dedicated to the literature art and culture of the East, and the *Poetryzine* - an online magazine for poetry in English. As an acclaimed and awarded writer, she has published her works in notable Serbian and international print or online magazines, literary blogs and portals. She is a member of the Association of Writers of Serbia, the Association of Literary Translators of Serbia, the Association of Journalists of Serbia and the International Federation of Journalists (IFJ), and in 2018 she established the Association 'Alia Mundi' for promoting cultural diversity.
E: anastyelya@gmail.com

MY CULTURE IS MY NEST

My culture is my nest
And I am a little bird
That cannot survive without its nest.

My identity lies between my own self
and the culture I belong to.

Like an artist and its canvas
Like a writer and its quill
This is the unbreakable bond.

With an invisible umbilical cord
I am connected to my culture
That builds my identity,
Brick by brick,
Until it builds a castle of my dreams
Drop by drop,
Until it fills the ocean of my life.

Thinking of my culture
I pay tribute
To all those great men and women of my kin
Who left an indelible mark in the history.
Who am I not to follow them?
To leave them and go?
No, this cannot be.
Ever.
As my culture is the feast for my soul
That floats somewhere beyond the vast skies,
Virtuous and immortal.

Nivedita Karthik
INDIA

Nivedita is a graduate in Immunology from the University of Oxford. She is an accomplished Bharatanatyam dancer and published poet. She also loves writing stories. Her poetry has appeared in *Glomag, The Society of Classical Poets, The Epoch Times, The Bamboo Hut, Eskimopie, The Sequoyah Cherokee River Journal, The Ekphrastic Review,* and *Visual Verse*. Nivedita also regularly contributes to the open mics organized by Rattle Poetry. She currently resides in Gurgaon, and works as a scientific and medical editor/reviewer.
E: nivedita5.karthik@gmail.com
W: www. justrandomwithnk.com
YouTube: @JustrandomwithNK

SARI

Six yards of elegance in one swish length
screams, no whispers, of tales of great strength.
It has no zipper, no hook, no button, no seams,
yet the sari is the stuff of couture dreams.

Chiffon and satin and cotton and silk,
there are so many fabrics of such great ilk
that it is the perfect outfit to take you from morning to evening
as this delicate drape has such a wealth of meanings.
Selecting a sari is more that simply a matter of choice
for each different sari indicates emotions from sorrow to anger,
ending in rejoice.

And through it all, the Indian woman stands strong
draped in six yards of eternal elegance.

INDIA IS MORE THAN

just the Taj Mahal and New Delhi
        more than Mumbai and Rajasthan
just saris and lehengas
        more than toe rings and mangalsutras
just Hindi and Sanskrit
        more than Tamil and Marathi.

India is about

the varied landscape
the richness of history
cultures and customs
us, the people.

INDIA IS POETRY IS INDIA

From the Vedic chants
      to the rhythmic qawwalis.
From the Bhagavad Gita
      to the Ramayana and Mahabharata.
From the morning prayers in temples
      to the evening calls of the muezzin.
From the daily morning pujas at home
      to the evening sloka sessions at dusk.
Poetry winds around us like the coils of the Adisesha
and is woven into our DNA, tight, like the matted locks of Shiva.

Poetry flows through our veins
and is writ on our brains.

Yesterday, today, tomorrow
Past, present, future.

It is all around us
We are all around it.
Poetry is us
We are poetry.

Ayesha Khurram
PAKISTAN

Ayesha is a 16 year-old student. She has been writing poems as a hobby since the age of nine. She admires poets like Wordsworth and Robert Frost, and has great love for people who write. Her favourite topics are the adversities of life, and humanity. She is ambitious and passionate about her poetry, and has won many prizes in school for her work.
E: ashiak7786@gmail.com

HER BEWITCHING BEAUTY

She walked miles across the sand dunes,
Her veil couldn't hide her beautiful eyes,
They were sparkling like little Jewels,
The sand was gently carving her footprints,
Her bangles struck gently with each other,
"She's beautiful" the winds whispered to one another,
She held a heavy pitcher on her shoulder,
No regret or tiredness! No weariness or anger!
The water in the pitcher danced to the tune of the breeze,
Her slender body and almond eyes resembled a cat Siamese,
The winds were blowing hard spreading the rumour,
"She is an enchantress who can see the future!"
The appearance of the desert was that of a crystal ball,
She looked like the owner; the only fortune teller!

Rema Tabangcura
PHILIPPINES / SINGAPORE

Rema is a domestic helper in Singapore and started writing poetry during the Covid pandemic. One of her poems titled *The Beauty Within* was featured in The Substation theatre play called *allieNation* in November, 2020. She is also a volunteer team leader at a non-profit organisation called Uplifters; providing online education courses about Money Management and Personal growth for migrant domestic workers around the world.
E: rematabangcura@gmail.com

I DREAM OF A DAY

I dream of a day ...
where love in a family grows and never fades,
Where hearts continue mending
Not breaking into pieces,
Were closeness and reflections remain.
Where wisdom, trust and faith that was planted to each other, will
hold on until forever.

I dream of a day ...
where life extinguished hardships and sadness.
Where everyone will enjoy the life that they want.
Where everyone has their own freedom.
Where everyone is equal to each other.
No inferiorities,
Nor superiority.

I dream of a day ...
where carefree and innocent children enjoy every moment,
where they could be loved and protected
and not to be subjected to abuse and torment,
Where they can enjoy being a child.

I dream of a day ...
where woman will be treated like queens, loved and respected,
Not to be played off,
Slaved,
Nor abused.
Where they should be treasured,
but not as a possession.
Where they should be cared, held close, and treated with loving
admiration;
Where they should be looked upon
as a true gift from up Above.

I dream of a day ...
where everyone are equally treated.
Where Nationality , Ethnicity,
Age, Educational background, Family Status or Gender will not
hinder,
As we were Created and moulded with Heavens images.

I dream of a day ...

where there's no more hunger, sufferings, and sickness.
Where there's no more
disputes, conflicts, and corruptions.
Where there's no more wars between brothers as well as Nations.
Where there's no more pollutions
that gave disaster to Mother nature.
As Heavens teaches us to love each other,
And not fight with one another.

I dream of a day ...
where people can love and take care the world they live in
where people can walk anywhere at anytime without fear.
where people can breath freely
without hesitation.
where people embrace everyone with no doubts.
Where people live happily, peacefully and beautifully.

I dream of a better World.
I dream of a peaceful World.
I dream of everlasting Life.
I dream of Paradise.

Raji Unnikrishnan
BAHRAIN / INDIA

Raji writes for the *Gulf Daily News*, the leading English newspaper in Bahrain. She writes using her pen name "desert rose" abbreviated as ~dr, reflecting the fragrance of those blooms that show up once a year on the outskirts of the arid land where she lives.

E: rajiunnikrishnan@gmail.com
FB: @ Raji Unnikrishnan
Instagram: @raji111
Instagram: @a_de_sert_rose
Twitter: @rajiukrishnan
LinkedIn: @Raji Unnikrishnan

THE JOURNEY

Yesterday I visited the attic of my memories.
I picked up this stained picture frame
with brass decorated edges,
which held in tact an old snap
of a thin and lean girl, smiling so naïve.
Beaming so bright she stood
against a wooden window
beneath the green bough.
Memories ran down the ancestral home.
I closed my eyes and stood still,
for a while, and taking a deep breath,
I could smell the jasmine flowers
which adorned her tresses.
Bindi decked forehead, kohl darkened lashes,
religiously bound amulet on her neck -
that smile had a confidence
which wasn't bold but, beautiful.
The portrait had a magic, which
I could no more relate to.
So very me, but not anymore ...
Bygone days of yesteryear!
Sitting by the sill, holding the frame
I stared – deep into her eyes.
The 'muscle woman' that she is today!
I smiled again, but not naïve anymore.
Searching within, I trembled as I realised ...
it was just the ashes that remained.
It was scary to rake them up,
for the fear of hidden embers flaming up!
The innocent smile on face
it scared me and I turned my eyes away ...
The fire could burn all down
the new and the old alike, said my heart!
The journey has been long
from that girl to the woman.
While mastering the art of balancing,
life offered no choice but to be thus!
The woman moves on -
spitting fire and laughing loud.
But deep within, aching and craving
to be thee but none!

Kate Young
ENGLAND

Kate is semi-retired and lives in Kent. She is a teacher and has been passionate about poetry since childhood. With a love of art, Kate writes a lot of Ekphrastic poetry, and enjoys visiting galleries for inspiration. She also loves reading, dancing, painting, and playing the guitar and ukulele, and belongs to three poetry groups which have helped and supported her in recent years. Her poems have appeared in *Ninemuses, Ekphrastic Review, Nitrogen House, The Poetry Village, Words for the Wild, Poetry on the Lake, Alchemy Spoon* and two Scottish Writers Centre chapbooks. Her work has also featured in the anthologies *Places of Poetry* and *Write Out Loud*. Her pamphlet *A Spark in the Darkness* won The Baker's Dozen competition with Hedgehog Press, and is due to be published shortly. Her poem *The Last Stars* was shortlisted in The Poetry on the Lake Competition 2021.
E: kateyoung12@hotmail.co.uk
Twitter: @Kateyoung12poet

LOCH RYAN

Chasing forbears, I am drawn
toward the purple smile
of mountain trail to Stranraer,
where Loch Ryan's tongue
laps the womb of the bay.

The fit feels right.
My bones slip into its shoulder
as I roll each chinned pebble
across my palm and sense
the smooth churn of endless tide.

From the cemetery atop the hill
I search for the vault.
I trace ghost- letters of family names
crudely erased, weathered
by breeze, brine and eons of time.

Did my great-grandfather's boots
leave prints in this soil,
were his eyes blinded by promise?
I imagine him grazing the shoreline,
boarding the ship to Larne.

The dates are faint,
gaps where ancestors slipped away
on American land,
before Loch Ryan hauled him back
with a long-awaited sigh.

THE CUCKOO CHILD

Was that when the unfeathering began?
The moment when
cushioned down loosened itself
to suffocate a fragile love?

Was it in that split-second
that you chose to protect me?
You adopted the role of motherhood
while she folded herself away.

I know you blamed her,
our weakened mother
unable to control the boy
who slipped into drunken rage

just days after the leaving.
We all felt the sting of words,
the ooze of it fresh on skin
that simply failed to quieten.

Words can be dangerous.
My Gran always warned:
you can never unsay them,
never back-swallow the hurt.

Is that why her eyes gazed
past your stricken face
to a barren wall behind
asking for me, one last time?

FACES OF ANGELS

Watching her tear shapes
from folded paper
she is oblivious to her peers,
a study in concentration

all dimpled cheeks
and naive eyes,
a child's key to ensure
they will be loved.

She unfolds her snowflake,
disappointment falls to the floor
with snippets of tissue
and tears of frustration.

I cup my hand over hers
so the scissors glide smoothly,
her tongue clipping her lip
to the rhythm of the blade.

In time we open her craft,
it unfolds with her smile
into something precious
unique, like all the others.

We hang them from strings
criss-crossing the classroom,
thirty angel faces look up,
halo-mouths speechless.

Amrita Valan

INDIA

Amrita is a writer from Bangalore, and the mother of two boys. She has a master's degree in English Literature, and has worked in the hospitality industry, several BPOs, and also as content creator for deductive logic and reasoning in English. She writes poems, essays and short stories, which have been published online in *Spillwords, ImpSpired, Potato Soup Journal, Portland Metrozine, Poetry and Places, Café Lit, Café Dissensus, Modern Literature* and *Indian Periodical,* as well as in several international anthologies.
E: amritavalan@gmail.com
FB: @amritavalan

SWEET SIXTEEN IN INDIA

Love comes in many forms
Sizes packages
Every time it holds different expectations
People who woo
Hoping to find a love so true.

Nothing matters but
The heart shouldn't shatter
And trust is a must
And none should prioritize lust
Over love.

Indian girls are told
Like Victorians
To wait, to be courted
Not pursue.

As a result my first love
Or crush at 13
Never knew.

My infatuation simmered
Reached boiling point at 16
Then vaporized.
Young girls grow tired of waiting.
And other boys happen.

So I gathered up the roses offered
Blushing coyly
I did not realise my youthful suitor
Was as tongue tied and shy as me.
Till on New Year's eve, he plucked
Courage from desperation
And leaned over …
Sensing the kiss imminent
I recoiled in horror
And tapped him over the pate
Smartly.
He recoiled like a revolver
With shot unfired
To his end of the sofa.
Then with a last ditch attempt at dignity

Apologised to me,
Took my hand as we left for the dance.
Concession to our evolving nineties
Modernity.

I think, I wonder still,
What would have happened
If I had allowed that kiss
At sweet sixteen?
He was dear to me,
So,
I rather suspect,
I always will.
Wonder.

SARIS FOR MY SISTE- IN-LAW'S AUNTIES

It was I
Who got to choose
The "*Tvatto*"
The saris and other gifts
For my brother's would be in laws
The wedding trousseau for the bride
And her family.

I was twenty something, determined
To do credit to my family
I drained daddy's deep pockets
Buying the best, the latest, trendiest
Silk *Valkalams, Kanjivarams* for
Pretty sister-in-law to be,
And crisp silk *Garads* for the mother
And aunties.

As a safe guard I invited my brother's
Fiancée to check out the saris for the elders.
She was very happy till she saw the creamy silk *Garad*
Picked out in a deep crimson border.
Horrified she raised her eyes and asked,
"Is this for my mother?"

"No," I assured her, her mother's sari was
Grander,
This was for her favourite ebullient aunt,
A widow.

And then, the penny dropped,
Mortified, I blushed.

Widows in India even now,
Even in families of educated affluence
Still wear plain white, and off white shades.
Bridal reds denied. Too festive, too libertine
Too loud.

I had forgotten, because my *dida*
Was truly modern, and she never seemed
Mournful in chic chiffons and silks,
But now I remembered.

Her saris were always in pastel shades, with
Slim borders, in blues and browns,
Never the bridal red.

I promised to exchange the cream *Garad* sari
With one of a different border.
As she left, I held up the thin red thread up
In my palms, catching sparkling sunlight
And shed a deep breath.
For the widows, our own mothers and aunts
Who are so vibrant, and yet,
Already supposed to be dead.

NOTES:
Tvatto: Indian Wedding Trousseau
Garads, Valkalams, and Kanjivarams: Different types of Indian traditional saris
Dida: Grandmother

Alicia Minjarez Ramírez
MEXICO

Alicia is an internationally renowned Mexican poet, translator, singer, university professor and broadcaster for radio and TV. She has won numerous international awards including: Honorary Doctorate granted by the International Forum of Creativity and Humanity, Morocco, and A Thousand Minds for Mexico Association; The Prize for cultural excellence (2020), awarded by the government of Peru; The Nobel Laureate Kobi Rabindranath Tagore Award, India (2019); The Excellence Prize in the World Poetry Championship Romania, (2019), and many others. Alicia is the author, co-author and translator of 17 international poetry books, and her book: *Moon Chant* in bilingual version, was recognized as Hispanic Cultural Heritage, and it is in the Library of Congress of the United States. She speaks French, English, Italian and Spanish, her poems have been translated in 20 languages and published in more than 300 anthologies, magazines and newspapers around the world.
E: minjarezalicia@yahoo.com

UNDER THE SKIN OF CHESTNUTS

Where the murmur of the zephyr
Turns into a song
The brush of branches on the horizon
And the swallow spreads its feathers,
Silent prayers perfume the air,
As volatile column of incense
Returns to celestial vault.

Each drop of rain
Suspends - exempts
Ostensible breath
Lavender and Roses
In random transit
From heaven to earth.

Perennial murmur
Germinates its song
Under the wet skin of chestnuts,
While noise purifies sleeping souls
Occlude - open eyes and ears
To the fertile seed awakens gradually
The tactile fragrance of the zephyr.

SYLLABLES OF FIRE

Languish the obelisk of my body,
As thirsty night of clarity
Reflects its roots.

Moisten labyrinths
As sand precipitates
Springs without confines,
Beating the silent voice of the waves.

Come, inhabit the instant pending of the air,
Where my heart burns and sings,
Invoking the nocturnal psalm,
The golden aura of your chest
Under syllables of fire.
Do you flow in my veins like God in rivers?

Blur luminous foliage of my oaks,
Dissolve drizzles,
Ascend - descend inebriations,
Intimate citric mist that from desire is born.

Come, navigate nocturnal emanations
Like voluptuous infinity
Detaches itself among the swell,
Incinerating enraptured echoes
Of my womb of honey and moon.

ONEIRIC SEAS
Translated by: Alaric Gutiérrez

The skyline
Outlines the trace
Of reluctant springs.
Gulls and sparrows
Silhouettes transposing
Dream seas of desire.

As a wounded reflection
It flows in the attempt.
Succession and extract.
Stroke that burns
Through my fingers.

Maja Herman-Sekuli
SERBIA

Maja is an internationally published Serbian-American author of twenty-two books. She is an acclaimed and award-nominated poet, novelist, essayist, bilingual scholar, and translator and recently she was chosen by the UN World Literary Forum as their International Ambassador of Peace; by the World Literature India as their Ambassador of Culture and Good Will; and by Global Literary Society as their Global Poetry Icon and Icon of Style of Serbia. In 2019-20 she was awarded 11 international poetry awards in India, Italy, Turkey and Romania, and the First Serbian Oscar for popularity. She is a member of American and Serbian PEN, American Academy of Poets, Association of Writers of Serbia and the Serbian Literary Society. In 2020 Maja was awarded the Light of Galata, from Mr. Osman Öztürk, President of Istanbul Arts, Culture and Tourism Association, recognising distinguished artists and people of culture who have been a sparkling light in the fields of poetry, arts, literature and culture.

E: maja.hermansekulic@gmail.com
FB: @maja.hermansekulic

REASON FOR THE RAIN

There was all this talk about Boticelli.
There was all this wine in our veins.
There was all this rain.
And all those people coming and going
Through my brain
Dancing on the ferry to another shore
Changes of scenery, of geography
Changes of heart
And there was this wall between words,
Erected with pain.
Will this rain ever stop?
Will the summertime
Open a window
And let the sun shine
From inside
Through my eyes again
After all these years
Of waltzing all alone
All by myself
Amidst the crowds?

OH HOW I LOVE THE SCENT OF AIR AFTER THE RAIN
For my parents

Before a cloud
Turns into a rain
It is fragrance free,
Weightless,
Floating
Up in the skies.
And I always can feel the storm coming
Even before it rains
In my veins.
When the cloud becomes the rain
It is water
But it carries the memory of sky
Of its weightlessness
Of it being air
And as rain it falls and falls
On the earth
On our shoulders
And in each drop
It carries
An inverted image
Of reality
Of the earth
Of ourselves.
Oh how I love that scent of the air after the storm.

My mother liked to bathe
In the heavy rain
Water mixing with water
In her hair
As if made of waves
Her divine beauty
Rising out of seafoam
Venera like
But so very human
To the red blood cells.

My father, on the Naked Island*,
Alone crushed a stone
With naked hands
Crushed it to the blood
In the rain or a storm

The water flew down the rocks
Mixing with the blood from his vein
Until his blood became
Stonelike, divine,
And lifted him
Thus, with bare arms
To take off his burden
To make him weightless
To wash off the blood stains
To fly him
Mythical
Free
Straight to the sky

Now I sit alone
At the seaside
Naked Island on my mind
Rain drops
Dig tiny craters
In the sand
I read clouds
As a destiny
Stones by the shore
Are most beautiful after the rain
Colours and smells are stronger then.

Oh how I love that smell of freshness
After the storm,
The mix of geosmin and ozone
Has its Greek name -
Petrihor,
From ihor - blood, and petra – stone
The name of that stone-like blood
Or, blood made of stone,
That flows in veins
Of their mythological Gods.

*Name of the island in the Adriatic where the political enemies were sent 1948-1954 under Tito's regime.

Maria Editha Garma-Respicio

HONG KONG / PHILIPPINES

Maria's journey with writing started during her primary school years. Nature and family serve as her inspiration. She has been working in Hong Kong for almost two decades, and is a member of various poetry platforms, and a regular contributor to many international magazines. She co-authored the anthologies including *Metaphors Of Life, One Tea in a Rainy Day, Love Letters, Adversity, Saving The World, One Poem at Time, All I Want for Christmas,* and *World Poetry*.

E: garmaedith8@gmail.com
FB: @editha.g.respicio

THE FIRSTBORN

Born near the pristine river and mountains
where ephemeral moments
spent close to nature
and countless blissful days
playing underneath the crimson sky.
Raised from a conventional family
where fathers toil under the scintillating sun
where fathers are assiduous blacksmiths, as well
while mothers are home-makers
and doors are open to neighbours
and extended family members
Twenty-four hours a day

Blessed to be the firstborn
and as expected, if I come of age
I will carry the responsibility
of sending my siblings to school
supporting parents, grannies
uncles and aunties, who are less fortunate
but I am cheerful to work
even if across the globe
it's a joy to be the breadwinner
for that's my manifestation of love
that's an oldest child's role
in my home country
The Pearl Of The Orient Sea!

Brajesh Singh
INDIA

Brajesh is a writer, poet and translator, and completed his Postgraduate from Lucknow University. His poems appeared in the international anthology *Ancient Egyptians, Modern Poets* and in a number of online magazines and journals including *Atunis Galaxy Poetry*. His Hindi articles, poems, and translations have been published in *Sahitya Kunj, Hastakshar*, and daily newspapers, and he is a member of the editorial team of the Kritya International Poetry Festival.

E: bsingh.idup@gmail.com
FB @Brajesh Singh

ZEPHYR

A svelte princess on a winged chariot
comes with dawn light from the blue sky,
recites verses under the swaying tree,
with nightingales and hovering butterflies.

Fingering the hair of a smiling child
under the shadow of a motherly lap,
peeks the rosy cheeks of veiling bride,
Caresses the hands of the labourer
and cherishes sweaty farmers,
in fields near an agrestic hamlet.

Slowly walks on undulated sand of Thar
with the humming insects at twilight,
and on the rhythm of Pungi, Dafli, cymbals, Dholak...
dances Kalbelia near the golden flames of a bonfire.

Rides on waves of the Indian ocean
and duetting with ferryman in the night
on classic music of shining stars
with silvery Sitar of fair moonlight.

Breezes down from the Himalayan head
and waves of the holy Ganges sanctifies,
spreading smile of Indian cultural legacy,
the messages of peace and zeal of lives.

Flourishing crops, blossoming flowers
joyful weathers, vibrant colours
heartbeats of earth, the melody of life,
undoubtedly everyone's desire, zephyr.

NOTE
Thar- Desert, Kalbelia -A folk dance in Rajasthan, India.

James Aitchison
AUSTRALIA

James is an author and poet who lives in an old goldfields town. His poems have been included in Australian anthologies and many other poetry magazines.
E: jimbooks@hotmail.com

AN AUSTRALIAN VOICE

Our voices carry traces
Of the great dry southern land,
The rasp of ploughs in places
That know a drought's dead hand.
Hard as the ground we mine,
Each syllable wrenched bleak;
A rugged mountain spine
Heard in every word we speak.
You can hear the arid plains,
The sweet green land beyond,
The crackling bush fire flames,
Black hills when trees are gone.
Our sarcasm's wrought with heat
As dry as summer's height,
As harsh as every dusty street
And the call of crows in flight.
With every beer we raise,
We spill no words in haste;
Like precious water, saved —
Too little here to waste.

Dr. Rehmat Changaizi
PAKISTAN

Rehmat is a renowned multi-award winning international poet, and the author of *Mia Bella Dea, Bella Diosa*, and *Ma Belle Déesse*. He is also Chief Editor of the annual international poetry anthology *Whispers of Soflay*. He graduated in homeopathic medicine and in Law from M.I.U, and completed masters in Urdu Literature from University of Sargodha. His poems have been translated into French, Spanish, Chinese and Arabic, and his work has been published in a number of journals, magazines and anthologies at both national and international level.
E: drrezi@outlook.com

SAND SEEKING

I see desert
Everywhere
Desert of memories
Desert of wishes.

Great desert inside me
Greater than Thal and Sahara
Sand in hands
We continuously throw.

Shadows disappear
In the sand of desert
Leaving no sign
But only sand.

Ocean Mother,
Always calling
Her sons

Scattered Oceanids
We do not reply
Though we will return.

STILL

When soul scatters
No one sees
On the bench of loneliness.

Body becomes statue
Like old historian
But without soul.

Without fragrance
Dried flowers in books
Are only memories.

When soul scatters
You will see
Shadows of memories.

Like shadows on sand of Thal
Before evening
Engulfs all light.

SAND AND HER HANDS

In the ample desert of Egypt,
Everything is dormant, tranquil
Life slowly follows the script ...
Air in its awe, remains still
The sky is free of a cloud,
Life walks, pacing alone
Dessert animals calling aloud
They're free ... dry to the bone!
A couple of thirsty lovers
Skim each-others souls ...
Like low flying plovers
Atop the suds-foamy shores.
Air moves sand at will
A lover uses a full fist ...
Spreading passion as a thrill
And scented love in the mist ...!
On all the vast dessert
Bellow the blue sky ...
The sun scorching oasis
Provokes the love to arise ...!
I open my eyes ...
My feet caressing the sand,
Was I sleeping in fog?
Was I holding my lovers hand?
In the wasted life of the dessert
My blood left stipples engraved ...
Marking the blue sky in my soul
With fickle scars well saved!

Alun Robert
ENGLAND

Born in Scotland of Irish lineage, Alun is a Kent based prolific creator of lyrical free verse achieving success in poetry competitions across the British Isles and North America. His work has been published by UK, Irish, European, African, Indian, US and Canadian literary magazines, anthologies and webzines. He is a member of the Mid Kent Stanza, the Rye Harbour Poetry group and the Federation of Writers Scotland for whom he was a Featured Writer in 2019.
E: alanrwoods@hotmail.com

KISMET HAS COME

he stretches out an arm
fingers profiling my face
scratching my patina
only sitting skin deep

he ingests my breath
rolls my damp lips
determining my diet
my predilection for drink

he listens to my lilt
inflections and stammers
searching for a heritage
only the deaf hear

he touches my torso
the frail and the fat
feeling for extravagance
beside the hunger and meek

he questions my existence
good and the bad
my honesty and fraud
like an IRS clerk

he looks me in the eye
close by my face
watching me squirm
as only the blind see

he ticks up the boxes
enters scores on a screen
applies an algorithm
to determine my fate

he points to the gate
I drop my head in shame
three score and ten gone
my kismet has come

Ion-Marius Tatomir
ROMANIA

Ion-Marius' poetic debut was in *Phoenix New Life Poetry* (Cornwall, UK), where he had poems published from 2004 to 2008, and from 2005 to the present he was periodically published in *Metverse Muse*, an international poetry anthology (Visakhapatnam, India). In 2006 his volume of poetry *Stars and Flowers* was published as e-book by L & R Hartley Publishers, (Australia). In 2010 he was included in *A Dictionary of Contemporary International Poets* (China), and in 2013 he was included in the bilingual Romanian - German edition of *Anthology of the Romanian Contemporary Writers Worldwide* (Starpress, Romania). Ion-Marius has also been published in France in: *Terre en poesie* (2007), *Paix et Fraternite en poesie* (2009), *Sourire et Amitie en poesie* (2013), *Tendresse en poesie* (2014), *Nuit et jour en poesie* (2015) and *Amour en poesie* (2016).
T: tatomir@gmail.com

OUR DUTY

With roots in Roman heritage
we are invincible bearers of Light
in all fields of science and art
traditionally dedicated to creation,
bringing sparks of innovation
not losing out of sight the essential
to be grateful to the ancestors.

To carry and keep alive the Flame
by serving God and Humanity,
Noble blue, yellow and red,
our flag and destiny,
Infinite blue sky, yellow wheat fields,
red passional courage and fidelity
the Romanian dream will ascend
and reach the stars gloriously.

Hand in hand, and heart to heart,
all around the world,
we Romanians are holding tightly the ideal,
to speak out, to feel what binds us,
what helped us to prevail
over the winds of historical storms,
the Sunday bells of the many little churches,
the stories about heroes who defeated the evil,
the traditions passed to the generations,
will make the Romanian dream forever live,
and our duty is to pray, act and believe!

Mary Anne Zammit
MALTA

Mary Anne is a graduate from the University of Malta in Social Work, in Probation Services, in Diplomatic Studies and has a Masters in Probation. She has also obtained a Diploma in Freelance and Feature Writing from the London School of Journalism. Mary Anne is also artist and has received multi awards and her art has been exhibited in various collective exhibitions both locally and abroad as well on line galleries. She is the author of four novels in Maltese, and two in English. Some of Mary Anne's literary works and poetry have also been featured in international magazines and anthologies including: *Barzakh journal of poetry, Literature Today - Volume 11, Flora Fiction, Litterateur Review, Poetryzine* and in the international anthology *Musings During a Time of Pandemic* compiled by Christopher Okemwa, Kisii University, Kenya. Her poems have also been translated into Serbian, and published in the official magazine of the Association of Writers in Serbia.
E: mariefrances3@gmail.com

Tempji Neolitiċi

It-Tempji u jien ilna neżistu.
Qabel kull żmien .
Iżda, huma jiftakru u jiena le.
Xorta għadna maħbubin.
Inroxxu fil-passjoni sa ma xi darba niftakar.

NEOLITHIC TEMPLES

The Temples and myself.
Have for long existed.
Before any time.
Still they remember, unlike me.
We remain lovers, drowned in passion, till one day I will remember.
Because the Temples know our story.

Meta jmut il-Baħar

Il-baħar.
Il-baħar hu mimli seħer u ċar bħal kristall.
Il-mewġ jitla,
mall-lejl, taħt is-seħer tal-qamar.

Il-baħar, maħluq għal-maħbubin, dak li hu magħruf u mhux magħruf.
Kutra li tagħti l-verita.`
Waqt li nixrob tazza inbid, niżfen mall-baħar u l-qamar.
B' hekk naħrab mill-verita.`
Għax naf li għada u l-jum ta' wara se jinbidel.

Naf ukoll, li meta titla x-xemx
Il-baħar se jegħreq fih innifsu, jinbidel fi plastik.

U jien ninħeba f' ilma oskur.

DEATH OF SEA

The sea.
A component of magic and crystal clear.
Waves rise,
over the night,
under the spell of moon.
The sea,
made for lovers, for what is known and unknown.
Possible coat covering the truth

I drink a glass of wine, to dance with the sea and Moon.
to escape truth.
Because I know that tomorrow and the day after will change.
I know that when the sun rises,
the sea will drown in her own self.
Transforming into deadly plastic.
And I vanish in dark waters.

Monica Manolachi
ROMANIA

Monica is a lecturer of English and Spanish at the University of Bucharest. As a poet, she has published three collections, *Joining the Dots* (PIM, 2016), *Fragaria's Stories to Magus Viridis* (Brumar, 2012) *and Roses* (Lumen, 2007), and her poems have been published in *The Blue Nib, Artemis Poetry, Culture Cult, Crevice, Contemporary Literary Horizon* and others. In 2018, she co-authored the bilingual poetry collection *Brasília* (PIM, 2018) with Scottish poet Neil Leadbeater. *Performative Identities in Contemporary Caribbean British Poetry* (2017), is part of her work as a researcher and literary critic. She has published numerous academic articles on contemporary poetry and prose including *Multiethnic resonances in Derek Walcott's poetry*, in *Ethnic Resonances in Performance, Literature, and Identity* (2019), and *December 1989 and the concept of revolution in the prose of Romanian women writers*, in the *Swedish Journal of Romanian Studies* (2020). Over the past 15 years, she has translated various types of poetry, as well as several classical and contemporary novels into Romanian. In September 2016, her *Antologie de poezie din Caraibe* was awarded the 'Dumitru Crăciun' Prize for Translation at the International Festival Titel Constantinescu, Râmnicu Sărat. Her most recent translation project is the anthology *Over Land, Over Sea: Poems for Those Seeking Refuge* (Five Leaves, 2015). As a cultural journalist, she has published articles in local literary magazines, and the bilingual collection of interviews *Table Talk* (PIM, 2018).
E: monicamanolachi@yahoo.com
FB: @monica.manolachi
Twitter: @MonicaManolachi

SMARANDA

I was on my way to the centre when I saw you.
The bus shelter had been redecorated
and your charming smile spread across the road,
replacing the usual street adverts:
a braided girl, enthusiastic and tenacious,
who broke the world record for parachute jumping.
Smaranda, where have you been all these years?
I am trying to unravel the stitches between us
and why I know so little about you,
although we spent our childhood in the same county.
The girl in jeans standing next to her chestnut horse
somewhere in California is not you.
In your fine handcrafted gauze cotton shirt,
you did more than posing for famous magazines:
you stood near airplanes to pilot them.
I see you gliding over glittering silver waters,
over Sacramento, Berlin, Bucharest, Rome, Tripoli,
brave and afraid, crying and laughing in the sky,
praying at 2, 6 or 7 km high in the air
like a white poppy gone with the wind.
Who can tell what the role of your poetry is,
whether it is mere décor or a world of the future?
When I dream dirty liquid bridges,
I remember this scattering of embroidered sleeves
and the multitudes of hands akimbo
scrolling down their smartphone screens.
Just because we cannot feel the future
does not mean it will not be.
Our life depends on the right stitches
between the big nothing and the small something.
Condemned *in absentia* because you protested
against the fraudulent 1946 election results,
cast out and buried too soon under a different name,
you have lain hidden like a solitary firefly
among the shady weeds of history.
I understood early that behind closed doors
not only good things occur:
abuse may also happen behind arched windows.
Very beautifully arched windows.
But a river like the Danube knows her kin
and dandelion florets freely spin
from epoch to epoch.

LA BLOUSE ROUMAINE

Migration, wars, famine.
Women did not have time for sewing.
There was not enough wood for fuel.
They lost their handcrafted blouses,
but they forgot neither their songs
nor Princess Ruxandra's sleeves,
painted on the church wall by Dobromir:
red silk and golden thread and love.
Let's have a coffee and tell me, please:
What's in a seam? Where can it take you?
National myths sometimes include a foreigner
wearing an embroidered blouse,
painted by someone born in another country.
And so a great number of artists
have noticed the dignified beauty,
the romantic turbulence, the concentration
and the feelings, the uncorseted bodies,
their calm and knowing gaze.
These exotic silent models
scythed wheat and peeled corn
and attached poppies to their aprons.
They tended the sheep, watered the horses
and wove deep endless rivers.
They raised the flag, gripped the dagger
and introduced metallic strips into the fabric.
They sang and danced and wandered
and patterned every leaf and petal.
They taught their children how to pray
and fixed little crosses to the ruffles.
They dreamt of the dead, talked with them
and passed the shuttle from side to side.
They posed, felt how a peony grows
and tightened the joining stitch.
They did not see the painter's signature,
but they drew blackbirds on the snow –
Needle and thread, I wonder how you are.
What broken hearts are you mending now,
in what language and in what place?

Igor Pop Trajkov
REPUBLIC OF NORTH MACEDONIA

Igor is renowned international writer, film director and multi-disciplinary artist from North Macedonia. He has participated in many literary contests including 'Viaggi di versi' and 'Il mio libro,' and, as a film director, has made a number of short films, documentaries, music videos, commercials as well as one feature film. His theoretical works about visual arts and cinema have been published in universities including the Catholic University of Leuven and Harvard. Igor speaks eight languages, and his writings have been extensively translated internationally. He is currently working on his second PhD at the Institute of Macedonian Literature.

E: igorpoptrajkov@yahoo.com
W: www.pyramidusd.wordpress.com
FB: @Igor-Pop-Trajkov
Instagram: @trajkovpop

WATER

How big are those eyes
that you are carrying
while waiting
for the whale that is getting
that fish in his mouth
without regretting
for not knowing the South,
the fishermen and the
sunburned tan on his neck?
"Don't worry honey, I'll be back!"
- said the fisherman to his lovely wife.
He placed the beluga sturgeon
pulling out the knife
from his worn-out pants
he smiled at his only friend.
She paid the rent
while he was imprisoned for
those from Yemen and Afghanistan.
The sailor cut he fish
in 2 slices.
How nice – 2 sons are chewing.
The sailor admires
the Mediterranean Sea, the best thing
he could ever had, as long as the life was going.

First published in *Coalesced Child* (2021).

AM I THERE OR THAT THERE IS HERE?

There were some days as like
they never happened,
spent in watching TV
the political problems prevailed,
everything seemed too difficult.
I am one of those who want
to believe that they can be as they are not from here,
but then why those do not move away,
those of my kind? It is because
they usually cannot, weak
is their organism, they become ill ...
I have a soul too
and when the day is sleepy
when the dawn lasts forever,
I see those civilized landscapes
costumed period dramas or
tennis matches broadcast on television
from America till Afghanistan.
Disappointment eats the life —
I'm here- everything is futile,
but the need for civilization is too strong
as it is here in front of me. Or I am there somewhere
guest to the One who set the rule
so that the psyche of the children will not be for sale?

First published in *Bay in the Night* (Scribd, 2019).

Tanya A. Nikolova
BULGARIA

Tanya graduated as Technological Engineer from UFT-Plodviv. She has had three books published: *Blossoms* (2012), *At the gate of the dawn* (2018), and *Awakening* (2021), and is in the process of preparing and publishing her new poetry book *Aura of Feeling*. She is a member of Plovdiv Writers Organization, and has won a number of awards including Third Prize in the XVII – the National Poetry Competition (2021). named after the Bulgarian poet, literary critic and translator Pencho Slaveykov.

E: tania.nikolova.n@gmail.com

ANCESTRAL MEMORY

I can still catch the sound
Of the waves splashing
on the shores of the White Sea.
Hoarse whispers -
Ancestral memory.
Thracian ornaments in my hair
Tenderly cancellate
Songs and parables from my grandmother.
Where children's games are still alive,
Amongst olive plantations,
Along huge turtles.
In the eyes of the memories
The old imperishable pain
Still reflects.
I am the heiress of genus
From ancient Thracian lands.
My soul -
kenar from woven silk.
And I take unearthly lessons
From proud Thracian eagles.
They are the meaning and torch
In life of my time.

Miroslava Panayotova
BULGARIA

Miroslava graduated from Plovdiv University, specialising in Bulgarian philology and English language. She has published poems, stories, tales, aphorisms, essays, criticisms, translations, articles and interviews in periodical and collections worldwide. Her poetry collections include: *Nuances* (1994), *God of the senses* (2005), *Pitcher* (2014), *Whisper of leaves* (2017) *Green feeling* (2018), as well as two books with stories: *An end, and then a beginning* (2017), *Path of love* (2018) and two eBooks: *Laws of Communications* (2018) and *Old things* (2018). She is a member of the Union of the Independent Bulgarian Writers and a member of Movimiento Poetas del mundo, and is an ambassador of IFCH (International Forum of Creativity and Humanity), Bulgaria, and a coordinator in an international e-journal *Ghorsowar*.
E: miroslava_panayotova@abv.bg

PITCHER

I want to drink water from a pitcher,
in the room under the sun,
to the flowers,
water,
overflowing from the pitcher,
feeling the splash,
before the pitcher broke.
I want to echo the music
from the radio,
to lean against the wall,
under the shed with tobacco strings,
next to the garden.
I want to listen
in the breath of the earth,
to believe in its eyes,
to melt into it
moaning with distrust.
To get through the corn
and scratch my feet
in the soil and foliage.
Let the wind rustle
before going to sleep.
To look for the past in a dream,
non-existence - in the dark rooms.
To bring water from the well
on the path,
on the song on the path,
came down from the cloud
in blue and warm.
To bring faith from the well,
filling my bosom with stars,
hands with fireflies,
dizzy from the ground,
covered with leaves and plums,
fragrant rotten apples,
the Earth,
laden with blossom.
Where is the house?

СТОМНА

Пие ми се вода от стомна,
в стаята под слънцето,
до цветята,
вода,
преливаща от стомната,
чувстваща сама изплискването,
преди да се е счупила стомната.
Да отехтя музиката
от говорителя,
в стаята под слънцето,
до цветята.
Да се облегна на стената
под сайванта с низи,
до градината.
Да се вслушам
в дъха на земята,
да повярвам в очите □,
да стопя в нея
остена от недоверие.
Да се промуша през царевиците
и да одраскам краката си
в пръстта и шумата.
Да прошумоли вятърът
преди заспиване.
Да търся миналото в съня,
небитието - в тъмните стаи.
Да донеса вода от кладенеца
по пътеката,
по песента на пътеката,
слязла от облака
в синьо и топло.
Да донеса вярата от кладенеца,
пълнейки пазвата си със звезди,
ръцете си със светулки,
замаяна от земята,
покрита от листа и сливи,
ухаещи загнили ябълки,
земята,
отрупана със цвят.
Къде е къщата?

ИДИЛИЧЕН СПОМЕН ЗА БЪЛГАРИЯ

Ти никога, знам, не затваряш очи,
ухаеш на жито и слънцето в теб
се сипе на пити.
Земята в лъчи залязва в небето.
Люляно от мрака,
потрепва полето с гласа на щурци.
Прорязват те облаци - живи реки
и ситно те пеят,
с чекръка си ведър
пак виното леят.

IDYLLIC MEMORY OF BULGARIA

I know, you never close your eyes,
you smell of wheat
and the sun in you shower on pies.
The earth in rays sets in the sky.
Rocked by the darkness, the field trembles
with the voice of crickets.
They are cut by clouds - living rivers
and they sing softly,
with its serene wheel
they pour the wine again.

First published in *Ghorsawar*, January 2022.

Ewith Bahar
INDONESIA

Ewith is a poet, novelist, translator and essayist, and lives in Jakarta. She had a long time career in the mass-communication, radio and television industry as a TV host at *Television of Republic of Indonesia* for several cultural and musical programs. One of her poetry books, *Sonata Borobudur*, got a prestigious prize from Indonesian National Library as The Best Five Indonesian Poetry Books 2019. She has published nine books, in all genres; poetry, short stories, novel and essay. Ewith also loves teaching, and taught at the Communication Institution, Interstudi and LEPPKINDO, and a public speaker for communications matters, creative writing and bibliotherapy.
E: ewith2408@yahoo.com
E: edbawythona04@gmail.com
FB: @Ewith.Bahar

SAMAN DANCE

In wonderful Saman dance
A majestic Nusantara's culture
Gloriously performed evoking proud feeling
An Aceh's song and enchanting traditional tune
harmonizing the fast-paced rhythm
of the odd number of dancers' movement
on the dance floor beauty meets the cultural wonder
the loveliness amuses my eyes
when they gradually move faster in breathtaking harmony
joyfully smiling faces remind me to dahlia garden
aware of world admiration watching them
they retain their enthusiasm, the Gayo zest and profound elegance.

NOTE:
Saman dance is one of the most popular dances in Indonesia. Its origin is from Aceh province and well known all over the world. By UNESCO, this dance was inscribed in 2011 on the List of Intangible Cultural Heritage.

BOROBUDUR TEMPLE

I am shivered with awe
When climbing your stairs
feeling so tiny

Beyond the steps I just see majesty
an immense ancient temple
marvellously erected
reaching the sky

thirteen hundred years ago, under Syailendra dynasty
you're built with gigantic stones
by glorious souls
profound art and philosophy
carved faultlessly
on two thousand and six hundred seventy two
relief panels along your body
depicting life and multi-faceted human behaviour
lies an exceptional reflection of ancestors' insight

Borobudur,
not immutable but perfect
arousing admiration
you're just alone on the high ground
a tranquil Kedu hill
you just sit, meditate,
feeling safe and sheltered
with Merapi, Merbabu, Sindoro, Sumbing and Menoreh around
the enigmatic secrets reside in your chest
eternal, unrevealed.

NOTE:
Merapi, Merbabu, Sindoro, Sumbing and Menoreh are the names of mountains around Borobudur
Temple area. Borobudur Temple Compounds was inscribed into the UNESCO World Heritage Sites List on
December 13, 1991.

LIKE A RAINBOW

Under the same sky
We dream a life in a harmony
Embrace the love and equality
No matter what the skin colour, religion and language
The diversity just reflects the beauty
Like a rainbow
which its myriad of different colours
Reinforcing the elegance

I speak my language, and you speak yours
But the real understanding doesn't come from the words
I wear *kebaya*, and you wear *kimono, ao dai, sari, lamba* or *kanga*
Those identities separate us
But the insight, vision and dream unites
It's your sentiment that can feel this rainbow's beauty.

Kathleen Boyle
VIETNAM / ENGLAND

Now based in Vietnam, Kathleen Boyle (nee Dodd), was born in Liverpool, England, where she spent her childhood years before leaving to train as a teacher in Hull. Kathleen then worked as a teacher in Hull, Leeds, London and Carlisle, and at international schools in Colombia, Bahrain, Cairo, Armenia and Vietnam. She has written stories and poems throughout her life, and published a collection of poems about growing up in 1950s Liverpool entitled, *Sugar Butties and Mersey Memoirs*, as well as a collection of poems for children about a teddy bear called *Harry Pennington*. During her time in Bahrain she wrote *The Pearl House*, a short story which spans the cultural divides of Liverpool and Bahrain. While teaching in Cairo, Kathleen published her novella, *Catherine of Liverpool,* and while teaching in Vietnam, has published her recent book *The Storyteller of Cotehill Wood,* with her new book *Rosie Jones* due for publication July 2021.
E: kathdodd@aol.com

LIVERPOOL

I'm from the north of England,
Liverpool, to be precise,
Oh, Yes! The football team.
Well, yes,
The Beatles too,
Well, yes,
And *scouse*!
That's right,
Very nice, good for you!

Oh, and it's a melting pot of cultures,
A place where people came for refuge,
Irish, Welsh, Scots and many more,
They came and settled,
There are the Welsh Streets,
The Irish Streets,
China Town
And Scotland Road.
And the River Mersey,
Once a gateway to the world.

I left Liverpool,
But never really left.
My heritage is there.
And when I see the City from the River,
I see the new, but also know the old.

The smoggy, smoky place where I grew up,
The Liver Buildings black as tar,
The war blitzed City where my parents, full of hope,
Were wed.
The workhouse, where my granddad was abandoned,
As a child.
A refuge for the famine stricken Irish folk,
The quiet, rural place of long ago,
Where once a castle stood,
 Beside the water, picturesque.

The Liverpudlians are funny,
And capable of huge collective outpourings
Of grief, and love.

Not only football, scouse and Beatles, then?
That's right, there's more to it than that,
Although they have their place!

Aleksandra Vujisić
MONTENEGRO

Aleksandra is a professor of English language and literature, and a passionate writer of prose and poetry. She has participated in poetry festivals across Europe, and her works have won prizes and acknowledgements both in Montenegro and worldwide. Aleksandra writes in her native language and English, and her stories and poetry have been published several times and translated into Italian and Spanish. In 2017 she started a literary project in order to promote the importance of reading for children, and starting from May 2021 she is a member of the Association of Montenegrin authors for children.
E: Aleksandra.vujisic@gmail.com

COLD

Once again the summer leaves
and the curtain goes down.
The first yellow leaf
falling from the tree
is crying on the ground.

It is not the first ending
that took away the sea,
leaving my hands empty
and cold,
like they never meant
anything to me
the waves left me
with all the tales untold.

And it hurts - the regretful
winds already started their song,
the wild rain is knocking on the
doors,
and like a never ending aria,
too painful and too long,
I call out the Summer's name,
waiting to be saved by it's heroes.

Once again the summer leaves
and this time it feels like
I am getting old.
The first yellow leaf
falling from the tree
is leaving my hands empty and cold.

I SURVIVED

I survived somehow
Easily
Red scarf and shining shoes,
I survived like this
All the nonsense
That outlasted
Inflation
And war for peace,
Nation gone crazy,
And the last sad caprice,
And yes, I survived some kind
Of dinars –
Kilo of banknotes for a kilo of bread,
I survived mine and other people's
Joyful nightmares,
A sip of sadness for
a piece of heaven,
And yes,
I survived sirens,
The buildings were shaking from
indescribable joy,
I survived migraines
And other gifts, modest and unforgettable,
I survived studying with no electricity,
For completely unexpected exams,
I survived thunders
outside the storms,
My heart and other
 people's hearts,
And yes – I survived the whole
Of Yugoslavia dancing
to the rock'n'roll,
When the brain is
squirming and the spine
Is breaking,
Our people became
other people –
And the whole world went crazy.
I survived running from enraged dogs,
Cold hands on my body,
Ghosts chasing me
from the beginning

And the salvation,
And many other things that I would never admit –
And yes, everything became
Different – nobody's, mine,
Everybody's, yours,
I survived the invisible calmness
And the visible air –
And then – when I leave will you care?

Máire Malone
ENGLAND / REPUBLIC OF IRELAND

Máire was born and reared in Dublin where she worked as a medical secretary for ten years. She enjoyed writing fun poems for friends and family occasions from a young age, but it was only when she was married and moved to the UK that she began writing poetry and submitting to competitions and anthologies. She has had short story prize wins in *Debut Magazine* (Stale Bread and Appleskins won first prize), and *Scribble* magazine published prize winner short story entitled *Me Da*. One of her stories was shortlisted in Words and Women Competition, 2018. In 2019, a story called *Hungry Roads* was longlisted in the HWA Dorothy Dunnett Short Story Competitions. She was selected for a place on the Novel Studio Course in 2017 (City, University of London), where she completed a draft of her debut novel, *The Dream Circle*. Her novel has been selected as a Finalist in Eyelands International Book Awards 2019, and *The Irish Echo*, New York, published an essay about it. She is currently writing a novel about the Irish Famine which was inspired by her poem entitled *Great People of the Irish Famine* which was highly commended by British poet, Katherine Pierpoint in an open competition in 2005, and published in an anthology entitled *Vision On*.
E: maireowens@aol.com
W: www.mairemalone.com

DUBLIN WAS MY CITY

Grey skies above rooftops on wet Mondays
Blue on fine days over the Dublin mountains
That shouldered rows of terraced houses
Under the watchful tower of our parish church
Lanes opened to a football pitch
Goals hammered doors
Until the light gave way.

Children swung from bandstands in Stephens Green
Conjuring bright futures
In their lunch hour, students devoured sandwiches
Sipped Bewleys coffee,
Pondered politics within earshot of
Bronze memorials to socialists and poets.

Grafton Street, lined with shops, fiddlers and silvermen.
Over the Liffey to O'Connell Street
To spot the bullet holes in the General Post Office
Pop into the Garden of Remembrance to gawk at
The Children of Lir and read the words of martyrs,
'In the winter of bondage we saw a vision'

The Christmas bustle of Moore Street Market
When the stalls were laden with oranges and holly
The dealers selling 'cheeky charlie' puppets
 Lilting wit breathing out the whiff of whiskey and Guinness

Dublin summers, my father
Taught us to swim at Sandymount
My sisters and I were his
Three lovely lassies from Bannion
His three Bridgets
Daughters of Erin.
Dipping his finger into salt water
He sealed our foreheads with the triune god.
Slow motion propellers, his arms sprinkled a grace
He could never speak
Then leaving us in shallow water, was 'off for a dip'
Way out beyond our vision.
We feared sea serpents, monsters, the selchie,
Until he returned, our father and saviour.

Prafull Shiledar
INDIA

Prafull is an eminent Marathi language poet-translator, and Chief Editor of a well known Marathi literary journal *Yugvani*. He has three poetry collections in Marathi, and one in Hindi. Translations of his poems are published in many languages including Malayalam, Gujarati, Telugu, Manipuri, English, German, Slovak and Czech. He has read poetry in many national and international poetry festivals and literary events in India, Europe, USA and Dubai, and in 2013 he was invited for poetry reading in 11th Ars Poetica International Poetry Festival, Bratislava, Slovakia. Prafull has written short stories, book reviews, film appreciations, interviews, travelogue and criticism, and is the recipient of a number of awards for his poetry, as well as for his translations including Sahitya Akademi Award by National Academy of Letters, New Delhi.
E: shiledarprafull@gmail.com
FB:@prafull.shiledar

THE BAND
Translation by Santosh Bhoomkar

A musical instrument is
Handed over to each one

A trumpet of hunger
A Cornet of deception
A Clarinet of clarity
An ancient drum set with hollow back

Tingling of copper and bronze discs
Of ancient brass
Sweet and neatly cut
Earnest tick-tick of xylophone

Saxophone with shapely turns
is singing in a sexy voice
At rising and falling pitch

In the folklore air
The fluke of a flute
The tube is blown
Saying "Come and sing."

While blowing the bagpipe
Of collective tune all alone
the air in the chest is exhausted

Each musical instrument,
While standing alone
Is staggering
Trying to keep its backbone straight
With collective crutches

A hoard of street dancers
Rush forward and twist
Participating in the
Performing band

Is this the wind band?
That turns its back
With the direction of the wind

Or the Jazz band
Engrossed in itself

Is it a glistening brass band?
Or the poor band
Playing gloomy tunes
In the last voyage of an untimely death

Is it a headless march band of an army drill?
Or a vulnerable band of the orphanage
Silently walking through streets

A rock band engrossed and lost
A metal band reaching the cliff
Or the well-disciplined police band

Is this a branded band
Or an assembled band

There is no one in front of it
Nor at the back
It sounds all alone
It is giving background music
To the occasion of universal dying

Will the fingers of curiosity
Slide over these instruments
Sounding traditional tunes
For years after years

Will it achieve
the rhythm of the spring forth

This band
In the heavy pouring rain
Has came under the shelter of the eaves

IN OUR LANGUAGE
Translation by Dilip Chavan

To speak in our language
To speak in our language with our own people
To share our innermost feelings
with our own people in our language

To experience the warm touch
of our language to our lips
To melt down in our language
To merge into something
that has dissolved into our language

If offered a glass of our language
I gulp down all the water greedily
Just in a moment.

Tatyana Savova Yotova
BULGARIA

Tatyana graduated in Bulgarian philology and psychology from the University of Sofia, and now teaches Bulgarian language and literature from 5th to 12th grade. She is also the author of ten poetry books, three of them for children, and six plays for children and adults. She teaches at a children's theatre workshop and has won awards in theatre and poetry competitions in Bulgaria.
FB: @Tatyana Yotova

CARNATIONS WITH BREATH OF MERLOT

Carnations
Carnations,
With taste of Merlot.
Carnations,
With breath of Merlot ...
Stay!
Stay!
My late love, stay ...

Outline
My silhouette with Merlot lips.
The carnation is
My heart with the colour of Merlot...

Let it rain ...
Let it rain ...
And Merlot, and let it rain love ...

... I am on you, my hair undone
And the night is not dark much longer.
Who I am, why I am – don't ask,
But wanting you to stay.

Inevitably,
Painful words in one.
Carnations,
Wounded with tears from Merlot,
Maybe,
Maybe
The glasses search for wet drops ...

... And what, that destiny – fire dancer
The destiny captured me with the third role ...
My love as you are in the shade,
But my love is stronger than the sun.

Dr. Sarah Clarke
ENGLAND

Sarah lived in the Middle East for 15 years and is the Founder of Baloo's Buddies in Bahrain - a non-profit program using pet dogs to enhance the life and social skills of children with communication difficulties. When not working on large scale inclusive projects, Sarah enjoys writing in a variety of formats including children's literature and poetry. Writing primarily on themes of inclusion, mental health and the environment, Sarah's poems and artwork have been included in a number of international anthologies as well as poetry events and exhibitions in Bahrain.

E: sarah@dscwll.com
FB: @Baloosbuddies
FB: @@sarahclarke888

WHO AM I?

In my first location, I was just me
A Yorkshire lass playful, carefree
There were cries of "c ya", and words without t
People just popped-in, appointment free
Sarnies sandwiches replaced
Chip butties my hunger often away chased
Everyone chatted with strangers on 't bus
While teatime came early for Northerners like us

And then in the south, what was this I found,
A foreign land where my voice didn't sound?
For suddenly bottles with ts could be heard
Why dinner appeared in the night, how absurd!
Newspaper headlines changed from workers unite
To titles that spoke of privilege not fight!
Public spaces were silent, not a word spoken
This world seemed to me a little sad, perhaps broken

Down south was somehow a different race
Though my passport told me it was the same place
Nostalgia for the familiar was what our hearts chased
The pull of home was where we all raced
And then I found myself across the Atlantic
The hurdles to cross actually seemed quite gigantic
Suddenly my words were cute, discrepancies outed
Say that again, people often shouted!

I strove to uncover how things were done
In a land that centuries ago had begun
The climate was different, the culture diverse
I found myself learning new ways to converse
Stumbling along this way and that
Often falling on my face with a huge splat
For while we spoke the same tongue
My actions were often at odds with those I lived among

And then I moved to an oriental land
Where my otherness stood out, some activities banned
Unable within this society to communicate
The muddles I landed in could be quite great
Yet I found a way to happily blend in
And learned we had similarities that help us all win

Through what we had in common, we could much share
There was no need to isolate and at others stare

So I find myself long gone from the place of my birth,
Entwined with cultures that give my identity enhanced girth
At heart I'm the Northern Lass my family knew
With roots well planted as new branches grew
Sometimes I feel a pull as a puppet's strings
And sigh when up north where my soul gaily sings
For sure I'll never forget where I've been
But how I finish up remains to be seen

Shaswata Gangopadhyay
INDIA

Born and bought up in Kolkata, and graduating in Science and Corporate Management, Shaswata started writing poetry in the mid-'90s, and is now one of the prominent faces of contemporary Bengali poetry. Shaswata has exhibited at the Poetry Festival in Picollo Museum, Italy, and has participated in a large number of poetry festivals across Europe and the USA. His poetry has been published in all the major journals of Bengali literature, and has been translated into English and published in journals and anthologies in Europe, America, Asia, Africa and Latin America. His book of poems are: *Inhabitant of Pluto Planet* (2001), *Offspring of Monster* (2009) and *Holes of Red Crabs* (2015).
E: shaswatagangopadhyay@gmail.com
FB: @shaswata.gangopadhyay.7

POETRY OF THIRD WORLD
Translated from Bengali to English by Rajdeep Mukherjee

I am nobody, nobody at all
Just a cultivator of cotton belonging to third world,
His youngest son
I have grown up by swallowing the froth of sea,
On my burnt skin
There is printed the world-map all over the body

Hunger rises in spiral motion
Around my stomach

If you give me love, I'll multiply it three times
By sheer magic
And put it under your feet
If you give me hatred, if you offend me
From my top to bottom
I'll come back not to take revenge
But to my writing papers
And I will throw each of my poems,one after another
Just like daggers

Yes, all the boys of third world are just like this

Julie Ann Tabigne
SINGAPORE / PHILIPPINES

Julie Ann is a domestic worker from Philippines. She has worked in Singapore for eight years. She is a Team Leader of non-profit organization Uplifters, and a member of Migrant Writers of Singapore. E: jannesakura021115@gmail.com

IT'S JUST A COLOUR

Find reasons to love your colour.
You are always beautiful
behind that appearance.
It's just the skin tone any way.
Love is within you.
Do not be so disappointed
because you are different
from them.

You must be proud of.
Your race, your history and your signature.
You can walk above your head,
to flaunt that beauty in you.
Your character must be your best attire to introduce yourself.
Build that self confidence
 that is hiding for ages.
The run way is waiting for you, my dear.
Go on, walk the swiftiest sway
the extravagant catwalk
of your lifetime.

This is the story
you must tell
to your next generation.
How you'd battled
to be accepted in an era
where black became the colour of nothingness.
But you've won right.
You deserved to be respected.

Dr. Archana Bahadur Zutshi
INDIA

Archana has a Ph.D in English Poetry. She is widely published and acclaimed as a poet and author, and has two volumes of poetry titled: *Poetic Candour* and *The Speaking Muse*. Her poems have been published in national and international anthologies and journals including *All Poetry, United by Ink, Spillwords, Confluence, Setu, The Bilingual Journal, The Madras Courier, MirrorSpeak, Duatrope Poetry Blog* and others, and her poetry was featured by *Culturium* (March 18, 2019) on the occasion of Women's Day and Poetry Day. She is a translator of both poetry and prose from Hindi to English, and her essays in criticism are published as chapters in literary texts. Archana has won appreciation and commendable mentions in contests conducted by United by Ink, POEMarium, Asian Literary Society, On Fire Cultural Movement and My Words: A Renaissance.
E: zutshiarchana@gmail.com
FB: @zutshiarchana
Instagram: @zutshiarchana
Twitter: @ArchanaBahadurZ
YouTube: @ZutshiA

CULTURE SHAPES IDENTITIES

There is an ongoing cultural flux.
By the invasion of the perspectives,
The original gets diverted, dented a bit.
Our cultural construct in a meltdown
Is revived by ardent supporters.
In the mash-up trends, we find new emergence.
Cultural enhancement or ebullient celebration
Is all about the identity construct.

We need a sound soundboard
Our cultural heritage is the amalgamation
Of experiences, the perspectives
Like language it is always tested by times.
A track which emanates after several footfalls,
Our cultural construct is the nascent rootedness.
All sense of belonging, a space
Existing, immanent, undiminishing –
Just like the memories.

Culture exists against repudiation, in negation,
Even through the transformation of cities
And dwellings, culture breaks out in bursts of life.

Culture gives national identities
To the global exchange of thought, a contextual identity.
A national character which is bold
Identification, beliefs, traditions, attributes,
A general conduct of the folks.

Culture is preserved in dietary habits
In food, flavours, folklores, music, art and architecture.
If cultural footprints are erased
History is a mere record of chronology.
Culture is identity of the advancement,
The progress made by mankind.

Culture binds the global populace.
It repudiates all hegemony,
Culture binds people in a commitment
Of benevolence and supportive stance.
It ferments coexistence of all species
and race.

Culture can never be diffused.
It is the fire burning in each world society.

END

CULTURE & IDENTITY, Vol. 2 - USA

FEATURING:

Jan Ball - CHICAGO, ILLINOIS, Jeanine Stevens - SACRAMENTO, CALIFORNIA, D. R. James - SAUGATUCK, MICHIGAN, Kashiana Singh - CHICAGO, ILLINOIS, Michal Mahgerefteh - NORFOLK, VIRGINIA, Madeline Artenberg - QUEENS, NEW YORK, Donna Pucciani - CHICAGO, ILLINOIS, Carole Stone - NEW JERSEY, Joseph Estevez - NEW YORK, Krikor Der Hohannesian - MEDFORD, MASSACHUSETTS, Kate Falvey - NEW YORK, Mary Marie Dixon - HASTINGS, NEBRASKA, Nancy Shiffrin - SANTA MONICA, CALIFORNIA, Suellen Wedmore - ROCKPORT, MASSACHUSETTS, Louis Girón - ASHEVILLE, NORTH CAROLINA, Ann Privateer – CALIFORNIA, Ed Ahern – CONNECTICUT, Michael H. Brownstein - JEFFERSON CITY, MISSOURI, Carol Seitchik - BEVERLY, MASSACHUSETTS, Nolo Segundo - NEW JERSEY, Ruth Sabath Rosenthal - NEW YORK, Darren B. Rankins - LAVERGNE, TENNESSEE, Gurupreet K. Khalsa - MOBILE, ALABAMA, Pinny Bulman - THE BRONX, NEW YORK, Robert Beveridge - AKRON, OHIO, Peter David Goodwin - NORTH EAST, MARYLAND, Antoni Ooto - NEW YORK, Judy DeCroce - NEW YORK, Mark Fleisher - ALBUQUERQUE, NEW MEXICO, Sunayna Pal – MARYLAND, Margaret Duda - STATE COLLEGE, PENNSYLVANIA, Lou Faber - COCONUT CREEK, FLORIDA, Timothy Resau - BALIMORE, MARYLAND, Neal Whitman - PACIFIC GROVE, CALIFORNIA, Wilda Morris - BOLINGBROOK, ILLINOIS, Djehane Hassouna - PITTSBURGH, PENNSYLVANIA, Karen Douglass – COLORADO, Laura Blatt - PENNGROVE, CALIFORNIA, Alexis Garcia - NEW YORK, Joan McNerney - RAVENA, NEW YORK, Anne Mitchell – CALIFORNIA, Gena Williams - NORTH CAROLINA, Donna Zephrine - NEW YORK, Hanh Chau – CALIFORNIA and Mark O. Decker – DELAWARE.

Printed in Great Britain
by Amazon

76773647R00190